Nashville

Hills of Harmony

Nashville
Hills of Harmony

Introduction by *Amy Grant*

Art Direction by *Karen Geary*

URBAN
TAPESTRY
SERIES
TOWERY
PUBLISHING

A DIVISION OF BARETZ PUBLISHING, LLC

Contents

9

INTRODUCTORY
ESSAY

Amy Grant cap-
tures the essence
of Nashville as
she reflects on
the qualities that
make her city
great.

18

PHOTO-ESSAY

Nashville's finest
photographers
contribute their
most compelling
images to create
an enduring por-
trait of the city.

210

PROFILES IN
EXCELLENCE

Profiles of the
organizations that
have made this
book possible
weave an informal
history of the
local business
community.

284

PHOTOGRAPHERS

287

INDEX OF
PROFILES

The next time you think of Nashville, think of Sarah Colley Cannon.

Sarah was a woman who epitomized the city. She was a part of both the genteel, moneyed Nashville of Belle Meade and the country-and-western world of the Grand Ole Opry.

The daughter of a sawmill owner in Middle Tennessee, Sarah (OPPOSITE) went to polished private schools, and was formally trained in acting and comedy, both of which seemed to come to her as easily as her grace and charm. True, she could have remained the hostess of Nashville society, and she would have done a grand job of it. Hosting teas, attending country club soirees, organizing the garden club—those sorts of things would have come naturally to her.

In 1940, though, Sarah put on a gingham dress and frilly petticoats, topped off by a straw hat with the price tag hanging off it, and became . . . Minnie Pearl. On the stage of the Grand Ole Opry, she was everybody's country cousin—someone so homely, and so down-home, that she soon became the Opry's best-known and best-loved star. When she came on and yelled "howwwdeee" into the microphone, the whole world answered her with affection and laughter.

From the time she took the stage until her death in 1996, Sarah came to represent the best example of what Nashville is really all about: a person who moves in both the dominant societies of Nashville—highbrow and low-down—without condescension or arrogance. This was her genius, and this was her gift.

In no small way, Minnie Pearl helped put Nashville on the map by making it acceptable for folks from every walk of life to tune in to country music and embrace the sounds of the back roads and the hidden valleys. ⇨

Nashville

Somewhere, I'm sure there's an angel wearing a straw hat with the price tag hanging off of it, watching over Nashville's rise to prominence as one of the world's great cities.

Would Minnie Pearl know the Nashville of today? Would Sarah Colley Cannon? I'm sure she'd be right at home. Even though the city has grown considerably in the years since her death, there are still the two Nashvilles–the cultured and the country. There's the Nashville of old money, higher education, government, banking, insurance, commerce, and high-tech enterprise. And there's the strong presence of the music industry, with its dominant influence on world pop culture. Many Nashvillians move exquisitely through both of these worlds.

Nashville is a thriving commercial, governmental, and cultural community. Downtown Nashville is just amazing these days, with everything from Centennial Park and the Parthenon (recently refurbished) to the capitol and the Country Music Hall of Fame. Something for everyone.

Nashville is a relative newcomer to professional sports. First came the National Hockey League's Nashville Predators in 1998. Two years later, we were celebrating the arrival of Tennessee Titans football. We had to do some homework to get the hang of hockey, but football was already in our blood: Nashville has always been a gridiron mecca. This is, after all, the home of Vanderbilt's Commodores, and Southeastern Conference college football has been a manic thrill for decades.

But when the Titans took up residence in Adelphia Coliseum on Sunday afternoons, we came together as a community in a way that we could never have imagined. When it comes to the Titans, we're as undivided as you can get. Having a professional football team has made sprawling, modern Nashville into something akin to a small town on Friday night, with everyone turning out to watch the local high schools settle their rivalries on the gridiron. ⇨

Nashville

tretching the entertainment dollar has never been more difficult in Nashville than it is today. In addition to football, we've got a wonderful array of museums, symphony orchestras, dance, theater, opera, art exhibitions at private galleries–you name it. The Tennessee Performing Arts Center alone is the venue for some of the finest cultural presentations anywhere in the country, and it's complemented by a number of private clubs and theaters.

Naturally, there's plenty of music, downtown on Music Row and throughout the community. I entered the music industry when I was a high school student. A number of courses in school took advantage of the unique opportunities presented by Nashville's status as the home of the country music industry. These opportunities ranged from performance to songwriting to the technical aspects of the music business, all of which prepared me well for the career that I would enjoy after college.

There are too many music venues to mention, and it would be unfair to single out one over another. But I will assert that some of my personal favorites are more along the lines of what people refer to as "listening rooms." These are smaller, more intimate places where audiences might hear an unknown performer who's destined for greatness, or where established performers go to participate in songwriters' nights. These events, where you just pull up some chairs or stools and sit in a circle and play your latest songs–with nothing more than an acoustic guitar for accompaniment–are really very personal, very special events, and I enjoy participating in them whenever I can.

still live in the same general area where I grew up, and I see changes all around me. I've had the rich experience of knowing many generations of my family who have lived here–my great-grandmother, my grandmother, my parents, the four girls in my family, our children. When we get together as a family, we compare notes, and we talk about how Nashville has changed, how it's grown. It's become so big and sprawling that it seems like the city takes up most of Middle Tennessee, running all

Nashville

the way down through Franklin and Murfreesboro. The business community here extends throughout the metro area, and it constantly networks Middle Tennessee towns together into one enormous community.

One thing I love about living here is enjoying the countryside of Middle Tennessee, which seems to define the personality of the community. There are gentle, rolling hills south of town, and I think the people who live here reflect the landscape. They're endowed with a more relaxed attitude toward life, and that perception of gentleness is reflected throughout the community.

You see this gentleness in the beautiful old homes in the Belle Meade area, which grew up around the Belle Meade Plantation (which is a great place to visit). You see it downtown, which is filled with soaring buildings these days, but which has maintained a grace and charm lacking in other big cities.

And you see it in one of my favorite areas, the Hermitage, an area that surrounds the house where Andrew Jackson lived. It, too, is a fabulous place to visit.

A tornado touched down in 1998 and did considerable damage to downtown Nashville. It moved through Centennial Park, and it went on to knock down a lot of the really beautiful trees on the Hermitage property. Some had been planted by Andrew Jackson himself, more than 150 years ago. Rather than just saw them up and haul them off, one of the city's corporate citizens—the Gibson Guitar Company—salvaged the state's oldest and tallest tulip poplar, along with a hickory tree that fell near the grave of Rachel, Jackson's wife, and created a limited line of Old Hickory Les Paul electric guitars. I love the appreciation of history and our heritage that those guitars reflect.

Every year, during January and February, the Grand Ole Opry comes back home to the Ryman Auditorium, where it was born some 75 years ago. Every year, for two magic months, people are able to hear the old bluegrass and country music played the way it sounded when it took shape under the fingers and in the minds of the music pioneers. And it brings back memories each year—memories of the birth of country music and the wedding of the two Nashvilles. ⇨

The reason for this, of course, is that the Opry was created by National Life & Accident Insurance Company, which owned radio station WSM (for We Shield Millions). This insurance company thought the Opry would be a terrific vehicle to sell policies to the folks who lived within range of the WSM signal. So they put the twangy Nashville country music on the radio, and inadvertently helped to create a new segment of the music industry. The original Opry serves as a reminder that the business and creative communities in Nashville—old money and new dollars—have long been truly interesting bedfellows. It has been a marriage that has benefited both communities—and, hence, the city of Nashville—tremendously.

And now we're watching the offspring from this marriage—the Titans, the diverse and vibrant business community, the thriving arts and education sector, the charitable activities, and the dining and entertainment offerings— as they grow and flourish, all made possible by the marriage of the two Nashvilles many years ago.

Somewhere, Sarah Colley Cannon—make that Minnie Pearl—is mighty proud indeed.

Nashville

elcoming visitors to the Athens of the South, Tennessee's capitol stands nearly 200 feet above downtown Nashville. The classic Greek structure, with its wide halls and imposing columns, was designed by the renowned William Strickland and has been in continuous use since its completion in 1859–some 16 years after the city was declared the permanent capital of Tennessee.

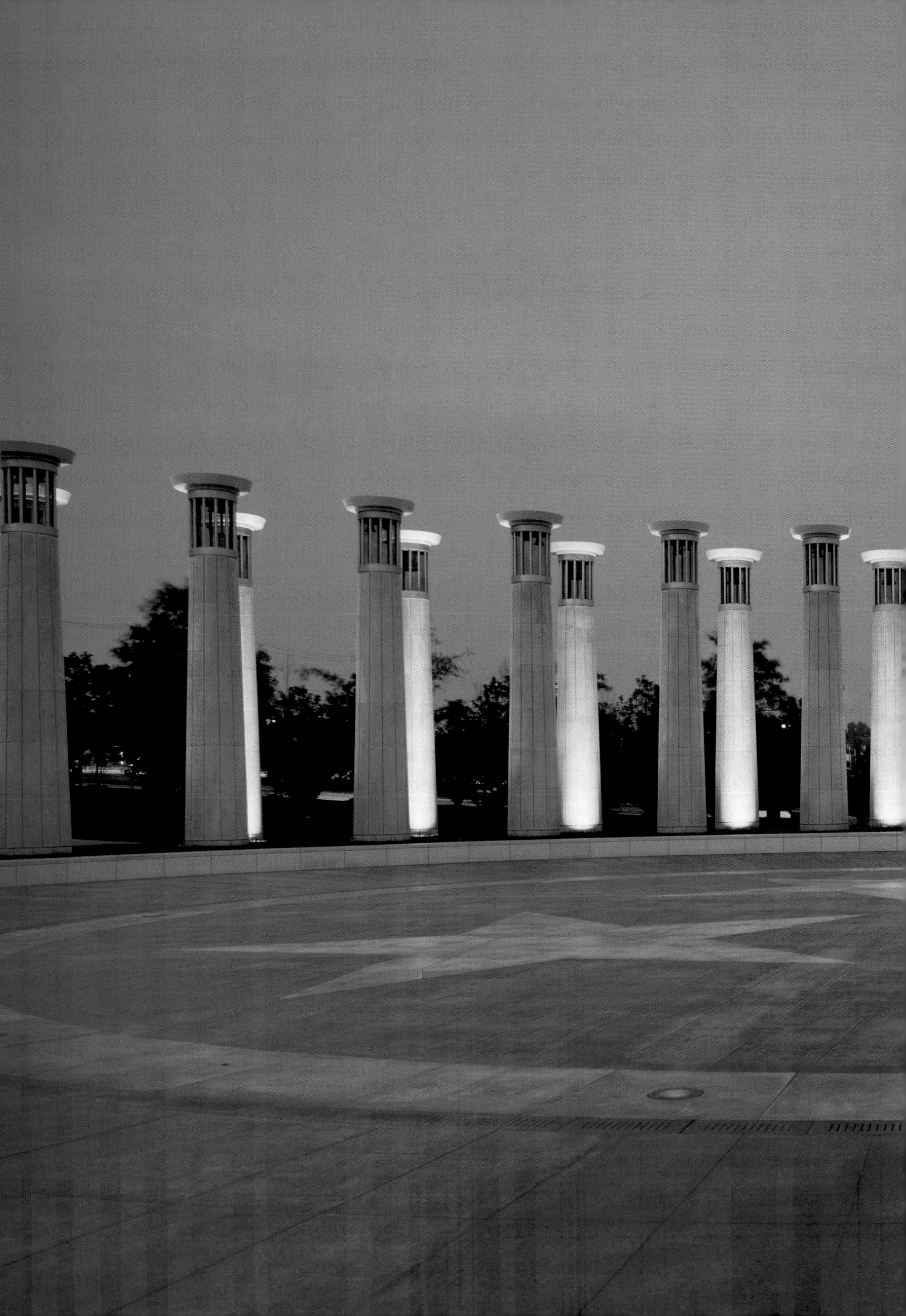

The Court of Three Stars at Tennessee Bicentennial Mall State Park is rich in symbolism, with three white granite stars in the center of the court representing East, Middle, and West Tennessee. Ranged around the circle's perimeter, the nation's largest carillon—made up of 95 bells, one for each of the state's counties—plays "The Tennessee Waltz" at hourly intervals throughout the day.

TENNESSEE
BICENTENNIAL
CAPITOL MALL

THIS COMPASS REFERS TO THE MAP
OF THE VOLUNTEER STATE
THE MAP IS TO THE SCALE OF
ONE FOOT EQUALS 2 1/2 MILES
OR APPROXIMATELY
ONE METER EQUALS 13 1/3 KILOMETERS
INDICATES THE OF THE COMPASS
THE OUTER RING OF THE COMPASS
INDICATES THE ACTUAL BEARINGS
FOR THIS PLACE IN NASHVILLE,
TENNESSEE

Since he was first elected to the U.S. Senate in 1994, fourth-generation Tennessean Bill Frist—a Harvard Medical School graduate who is board certified in both general surgery and heart surgery—has operated as a strong political compass on a number of points. Frist is a member of myriad committees and serves as chair of the Senate's public health and safety subcommittee.

Nashville

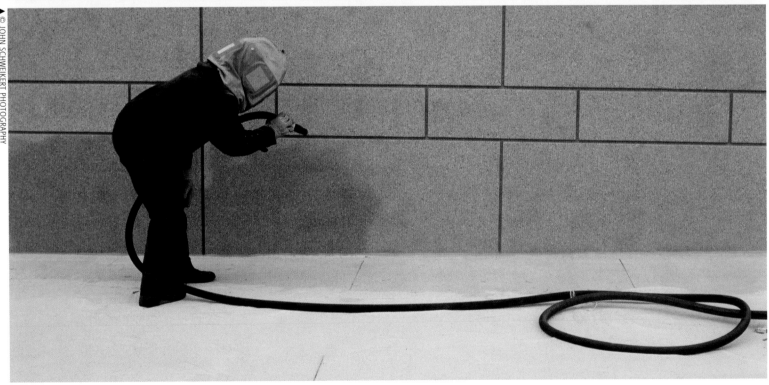

ake me to your leader: As the seat of state government, Nashville is accustomed to unusual visitors. Upon closer inspection, some appear to be alien beings, such as those lurking outside the Curious Heart gift shop (OPPOSITE) or swarming on the Davidson County Courthouse lawn (TOP).

*B*ill Purcell (LEFT), *the fifth mayor of the Metropolitan Government of Nashville and Davidson County, was elected in 1999. Determined to have his city put its best foot forward, Purcell has made Nashville's school system one of his top priorities.*

On the road again: Nashville's distinctive skyline greets commuters and travelers as they approach the downtown area.

*S*ince it officially opened in 1937 with two hangars and a single runway, Nashville International Airport has risen to the challenge of keeping pace with the ever expanding city and its surrounds. Nearly 20 carriers now serve some 8 million passengers each year.

Nashville

*D*esignated Tennessee's permanent capital in 1843, Nashville's continuous growth has long been reflected in the faces of those who hang in there to get the job done (PAGES 34-37). Nashville and Davidson County, home to some 500,000 people, now cover more than 533 square miles.

Nashville

*I*n the late 1890s, the
Parthenon in Nashville—the
world's only full-scale replica
of the ancient Greek Parthenon—was
built as a temporary centerpiece for
Tennessee's Centennial Exposition.
Converted to a permanent building
in the 1920s, it was one of the first
concrete structures in the country
and has been extensively renovated,
including new limbs for some of the
building's statuary (OPPOSITE). The
Parthenon, located in Centennial
Park, features the Cowan Collection
of American art, as well as artifacts
from the site's history.

Nashville

FOR SALE
5 ACRE
NO RESTRICTIONS
758-8908
230-1068

SEWER & GAS
HERE
YOU COULD DIVIDE
TERMS

N estled against a backdrop of rolling, tree-covered hills, Nash-ville's burgeoning suburbs combine proximity to the city's cultural and economic opportunities with a pastoral setting.

There are numerous ways to feel at home in Nashville, as the city's neighborhoods represent a timeline of architectural styles and eras. The city is home to Davidson County's largest surviving group of Victorian houses, in addition to a wealth of early 20th-century and sedate brick homes.

*T*he purple iris, Tennessee's official cultivated flower (OPPOSITE TOP), has earned Nashville the nickname Iris City. Far from a one-bloom town, though, Nashville is a breeding ground for gardeners who sow the seeds of variety, whether working singly or as part of a group effort.

*R*ush hour is an unfortunate fact of 21st-century city life, but seeing red is a little more tolerable when the color stems from bright poppies and other wildflowers planted along the medians of major thoroughfares. Tennessee's Department of Transportation maintains hundreds of blossom-covered highway acres across the state.

BELLSOUTH
BLUEGRASS INN
Robert's
WESTERN WORLD
JACKS
BAR-B-QUE
NASHVILLE GIFTS

Although the BellSouth Building maintains its constant, corporate watch over Broadway, honky-tonks like Robert's Western World and other hot spots take over the street by night. Robert's, which does double time selling boots and music, secured a place on the charts of Music City's unofficial hall of fame by fostering eclectic country music quintet BR5-49. The band has gone on to earn worldwide acclaim.

Just around the corner from the Ryman Auditorium, Tootsies Orchid Lounge and owner Colonel Bob Register (ABOVE) have hosted countless established musicians and rising stars. Those who have performed in Tootsies' memorabilia-bedecked atmosphere include Waylon Jennings, Patsy Cline, and Willie Nelson, who got his first songwriting job after playing a gig there.

Nashville

ACME FARM SUPPLY

PURINA
HEALTH
PRODUCTS

PURINA
SHOWS

*P*icture this: Street musicians in Nashville may provide passersby with flashes of local sound and color, but tourists are no less likely to draw the attention of onlookers.

*U*nion Station has been a haven for travelers through downtown Nashville since October 1900. Originally a passenger train depot, the landmark structure is now the Wyndham Union Station hotel. The facility features a vaulted, stained-glass ceiling that welcomes guests to the luxurious lobby with a historic flourish.

Nashville

*T*here's plenty to cheer about at the Opryland Hotel Nashville. Located in the heart of Grand Ole Opry country, the hotel features nearly 2,900 guest rooms enclosing nine acres of indoor gardens and a smorgasbord of indoor and alfresco eateries.

Nashville

In 2000, the Grand Ole Opry turned 75, proving once and for all that growing older should be a source of pride. The year-long celebration continued well into 2001, with generations of country musicians paying homage to the icon and some of its brightest stars. But the Opry name transcends music: Just seven miles from downtown Nashville, Opry Mills—a 1.2 million-square-foot shopping extravaganza—makes every day a party at its collection of more than 200 stores.

$\mathcal{N}$o reason to be blue: Since she burst onto the country music scene in 1996 at the age of 13, LeAnn Rimes (ABOVE) has captivated audiences with her onstage charm and garnered industry honors for her powerful voice. Vince Gill (OPPOSITE), who has won more than a dozen Grammys, received a Country Weekly Career Achievement Award in 2001. The award, presented to performers whose musical contributions span at least 15 years, confirms that Gill's fans won't let their love start slippin' away.

COUNTRY MUSIC HALL OF FAME AND MUSEUM

*T*he Country Music Hall of Fame and Museum has been a gold mine of American music since 1967. Its new location, which opened in 2001, covers an entire city block and includes 40,000 square feet of exhibit space.

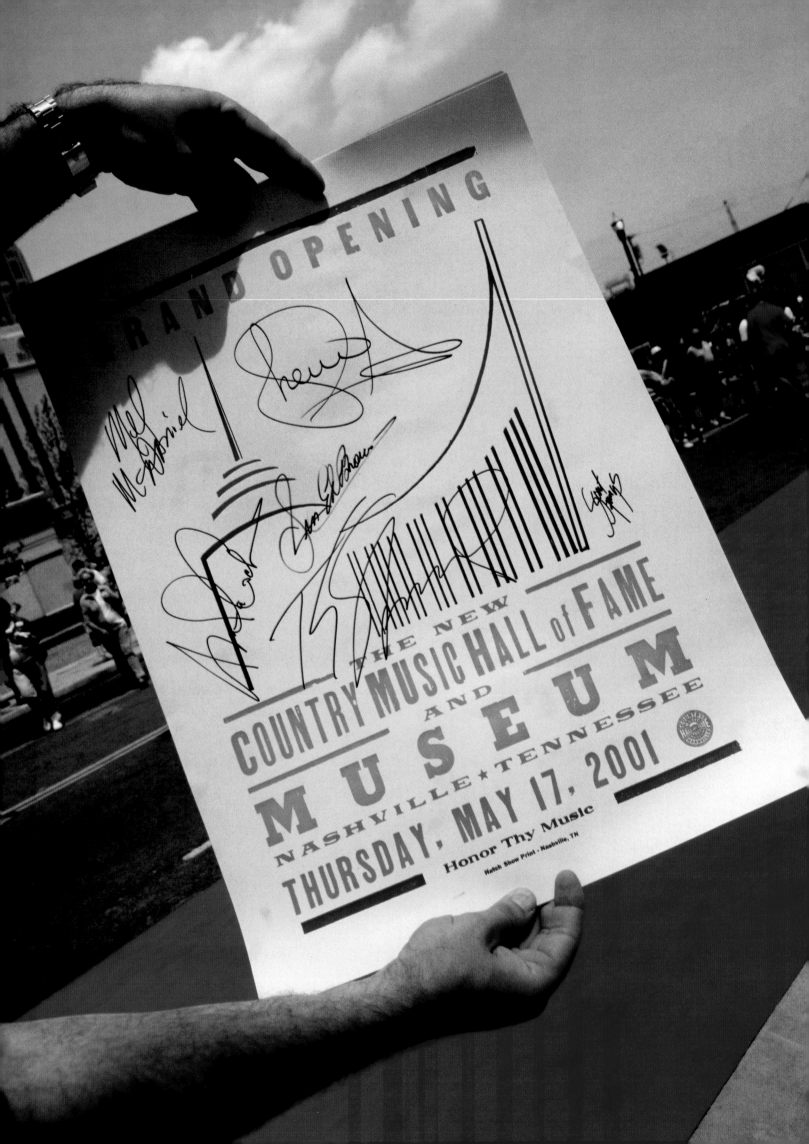

On May 17, 2001, Nashville banded together to roll out the red carpet for the new Country Music Hall of Fame. A host of legendary musicians—including Too Slim of Riders in the Sky (TOP LEFT), Brenda Lee (TOP RIGHT), and Marty Stuart and Earl Scruggs (BOTTOM LEFT)—performed and signed autographs for hundreds of fans.

Chet Atkins
June 20, 1924 – June 30, 2001

When guitar virtuoso and 13-time Grammy winner Chet Atkins left the Nashville stage for the last time in 2001, nearly 2,000 turned out for his memorial service at Ryman Auditorium, and legions of fans lined the wall outside the building to pay tribute to the songwriter, performer, and producer. Atkins is credited as the creator of the Nashville Sound that took country music by storm and revitalized the genre, transforming it into a booming industry and an economic boon for the city.

GRAND OLE OPRY.
GRAND OLE OPRY.

From third-generation
Opry denizen Hank
Williams III (ABOVE) to those
whose appeal and careers span the
decades—including (OPPOSITE, CLOCK-
WISE FROM TOP LEFT) *Little Jimmy*

Dickens, Roy Clark, George Jones,
and Don Everly—representatives of
multiple generations performing at
the Grand Ole Opry are living proof
of that institution's durability.

*H*atch Show Print, one of the oldest and best-known working letterpress shops in the country, has operated in Nashville since 1879. Now turning out some 600 distinctive jobs per year (OPPOSITE), Hatch can lay claim to a diverse clientele that includes Shania Twain, Trisha Yearwood, and Bob Dylan. Bryce McCloud–owner of Isle of Printing and a Hatch protégé–adds his own eccentric signature to everything from business cards to wedding invitations (ABOVE).

arger than life: From the more than 50 stars of the country music stage immortalized at the Music Valley Wax Museum (TOP) to a replica of the Ryman Auditorium's stage at the Grand Ole Opry Museum (CENTER), a score of exhibits help paint a picture of Nashville's musical heritage. For those who prefer to be on the scene when history is being made, the annual CMA Awards offer the opportunity to catch a glimpse of—or get an autograph from—luminaries such as Pam Tillis (BOTTOM). The Ryman Auditorium (OPPOSITE), built as a church in 1892 and declared a National Historic Landmark in 2001, has long been revered as one of the best live-music venues in the country.

*N*ashvillians know that, no matter what else, ya gotta have style. Shawna McPherson (ABOVE) lassos commissions with her bright-hued murals and canvases. Nathan Spears and Katy K Designs (OPPOSITE) stock a full closet of vintage and modern clothing, costumes, and accessories—many of which are created in-house.

Nashville

*I*n April 2001, the nonprofit Frist Center for the Visual Arts held its grand opening, chalking up an attendance of thousands of spectators. The building, which once served as the city's main post office, was renovated by local architect Seab Tuck, who took especial care to preserve the structure's Art Deco features. The facility house the largest art exhibition space in the city—24,000 feet—and showcases the work of regional, national, and international artists.

Myles Maillie

T *he Tennessee Performing Arts Center (TPAC) hosted the first Fest de Ville Nashville in 2000. The festival featured ethnic dance demonstrations, as well as artists—such as James Threalkill (ABOVE) and Myles Maillie (OPPOSITE, BOTTOM RIGHT)—illustrating their trade. Live performances by musicians including Aashid Himons (BOTTOM) and Jimmy Hall (OPPOSITE, TOP LEFT) also made a hit at the multiday event.*

*N*ashville River Stages has only been held since 1998, but the annual, three-day festival has quickly become a local tradition at Riverfront Park. Featuring a spectrum of musical names and genres performing on multiple outdoor stages, the event is a laid-back feast for the senses.

82   Nashville

*O*perating under the auspices of the Tennessee Association of Craft Artists, the annual Tennessee Crafts Fair offers a patchwork of handiwork for kids of all ages. In the shadow of the Parthenon in Centennial Park, attendees can peruse, shop for, and learn about art forms from woodcraft to fabric art.

FIRST
PLACE
4-H

AGRICULTURE

TENNESSEE
STATE
FAIR

Nashville

*E*veryone can find something
to get their teeth into at the
Tennessee State Fair. Taking
over the Tennessee State Fairgrounds
just after Labor Day, the fair's many
events include agricultural shows and
contests, arts and crafts, and a traditional midway bursting with food,
games, and rides.

What goes around comes around on the Tennessee Fox Trot Carousel in Riverfront Park. Created by internationally respected artist Red Grooms (OPPOSITE) as a tribute to his hometown, the carousel sports 36 fiberglass sculptures, each of which depicts a figure from Tennessee's history, from Andrew Jackson to Kitty Wells.

*W*hatever means they use to patrol their city, the 1,300 officers of the Metropolitan Nashville Police Department work not only to enforce the law, but to maintain active links and open lines of communication with the community they serve and protect.

A mere trot from Nashville, the Harlinsdale Farm offers a peek into the world of Tennessee Walking Horses. The farm was started in the 1930s and was the home of Midnight Sun. A two-time national champion Walking Horse in the 1940s, Midnight Sun is still spoken of as the quintessential horse of his breed.

he race is on: The Iroquois Steeplechase has been running strong at Percy Warner Park since the 1940s. The race usually draws a crowd of about 25,000. Most fans come to watch the historical event or learn more about racing, but a few opt to get their feet wet in a more literal sense.

Nashville

*C*apping off the Iroquois
Steeplechase, fans' exuberant
headgear and officials' costumes–such as that of George Sallee,
the race's horn blower and official
bugler (LEFT)–are nearly as much
a part of tradition as the horses
themselves.

Nashville

*R*espite from the buzz of the city is never far away in the Nashville area. Peaceful, tree-lined roads wind their way among the farms that dot the region, providing ample opportunity for a quiet walk or scenic drive (PAGES 96-99).

Nashville

he Nashville Farmer's Market sells everything necessary for enjoying a picnic lunch at adjacent Tennessee Bicentennial Mall State Park. More than 200 open-air stalls are abloom with produce, baked goods, meats, and plants to satisfy even the most discerning palate.

LIMITED FOOD SUPPLY
PLEASE TAKE ONLY
WHAT YOU NEED

Nashville

espite the uphill work involved, runners of all stripes compete for cash prizes in the Country Music Marathon (LEFT). The 26-mile race starts at Centennial Park and winds through town to the finish line at Adelphia Coliseum. At the annual Belle Meade Boulevard Bolt (OPPOSITE), participants in the five-mile turkey trot go bananas in a concerted fund-raising effort to assist the area's homeless residents.

What's in a name? For the Tennessee Titans, an AFC championship and a trip to Super Bowl XXXIV in 2000–after the team's first season as the Titans–were part of the package. At the postgame parade, defensive tackle Joe Salave'a showed his spirit by videotaping fans for posterity (BOTTOM). The Titans franchise, founded in 1960 as the Houston Oilers, moved to Tennessee in 1997.

Nashville

*E*lvis is in the ballpark: There's always a full house at the Tennessee Titans' home games. Since Adelphia Coliseum was completed in 1999, fans have jammed the stadium's nearly 68,000 seats for a chance to root for the home team.

Hills of Harmony

Nashville

*T*he Titans Cheerleaders do more than their share to keep the football crowds fired up. But for independent, over-the-top fandom, even the cheerleaders take their hats off to the Flameheads, whose fiery face paint and creative crowns mark them as true diehards.

Nashville

The Nashville Predators control the territory and keep the competition in check at Gaylord Entertainment Center, where the franchise has lured its prey since its inaugural NHL game in 1998.

*T*he Nashville area brings golf to the fore, giving aficionados the chance to putter around on the sidelines. Major events like the Electrolux USA Championship and the BellSouth Senior Classic draw some of the biggest names in the LPGA and PGA to the region, including (CLOCKWISE FROM TOP) *Pat Hurst, Hale Irwin, Gary Player, and Annika Sorenstam.*

Nashville

*B*aseball season scores a round of applause as the Nashville Sounds turn up the volume. As the Triple-A affiliate of the Pittsburgh Pirates, the team– with the help of its mascot, Ozzie– makes a hit at Greer Stadium.

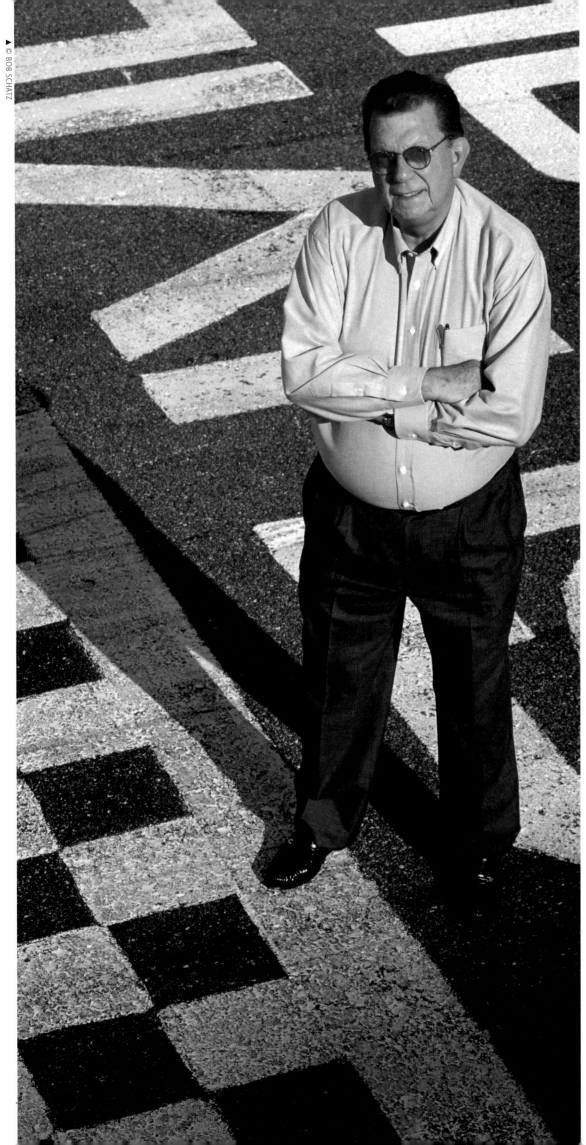

*W*heeling and dealing: Bob Harmon, president of Nashville Speedway (LEFT), *pulls out all the stops to keep the track on the NASCAR circuit. Although the speedway relies heavily on weekly races, it shifted into high gear in 2000 as host of the BellSouth Mobility 320 Busch Grand National– just the ticket for winner Randy LaJoie* (OPPOSITE TOP).

W hether for fun or in competition, in a residential neighborhood or on a park trail, young Nashvillians get on board for freewheeling athletic activities. Events like the Lock 4 Challenge (LEFT), an 8.5-mile race held at Lock 4 Mountain Bike Park in nearby Gallatin, offer participants a chance to put the pedal to the metal.

Nashville

*V*olunteers and other staff members at the Metro Greenways Commission take justifiable pride in their work, carving out spots for relaxation and education within the city's borders. At Shelby Bottoms Greenway and Nature Park, seasonal cycles are visible everywhere, from the 10 miles of trails to the scenic overlooks scattered throughout the 810-acre park. Located in East Nashville, Shelby Bottoms is connected to downtown—not quite four miles away—by the Davidson Street Bicycle Connector.

rching high over Highway 96 in Franklin, Tennessee, the Natchez Trace Bridge provides a singular view of breathtaking vistas along the Natchez Trace Parkway, a 442-mile roadway that stretches from Natchez to Nashville.

Nashville

*O*utdoor beauty and recreation are always in season in the Nashville region, with brilliant leaves and snow-covered trees allowing residents to slide effortlessly from autumn into winter.

*W*ith its vast array of name-brand equipment, Walter Nipper's Nashville Sporting Goods Company in down-town Nashville reels in sports buffs hand over glove. At Percy Priest Lake (OPPOSITE), under the hopeful glow of the rising sun, the early bird casts the worm in anticipation of catching some striped bass.

NASHVILLE

SPORTING

GOODS

POST SIGN CO.

WALTER NIPPER'S

Nashville

H i l l s   o f   H a r m o n y

Nashville

ently down the stream: The Harpeth River (OPPOSITE), which flows through Davidson County, is just one of the region's many navigable waterways. On days when the world looks best from a distance, kayaks and other watercraft allow residents and visitors to leave it all behind.

*S*trange creatures of all kinds find their way into Tennessee's many parks and watering holes, from the local beauty of Beaman Park (LEFT) to the peaceful Big South Fork National River and Recreational Area (OPPOSITE), a few hours' drive from the city.

*R*ipple effect: With water, water everywhere, Nashville's youth are never up a creek when it comes to finding places to play.

part from the statuary, very little is set in stone at Cheekwood Botanical Garden and Museum of Art, which contains myriad, dazzling gardens that change their displays with the seasons. At Owl's Hill Nature Center (TOP), a 150-acre nature sanctuary owned by Cheekwood, guided tours offer lessons about conservation and species protection.

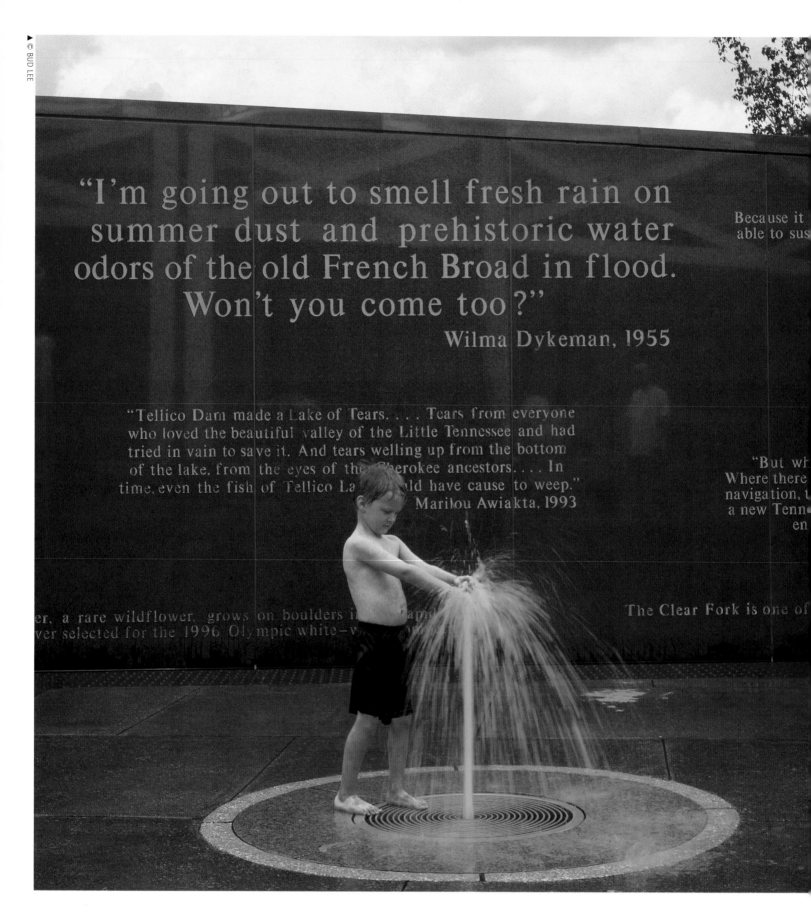

"I'm going out to smell fresh rain on summer dust and prehistoric water odors of the old French Broad in flood. Won't you come too?"

Wilma Dykeman, 1955

Because it able to sus

"Tellico Dam made a Lake of Tears. . . . Tears from everyone who loved the beautiful valley of the Little Tennessee and had tried in vain to save it. And tears welling up from the bottom of the lake, from the eyes of the Cherokee ancestors. . . . In time, even the fish of Tellico La ld have cause to weep."

Marilou Awiakta, 1993

"But wh Where there navigation, a new Tenne en

er, a rare wildflower, grows on boulders i ap ver selected for the 1996 Olympic white-v

The Clear Fork is one o

Nashville

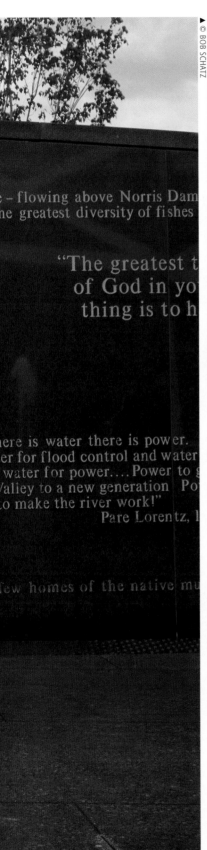

- flowing above Norris Dam
he greatest diversity of fishes

"The greatest t
of God in yo
thing is to h

ere is water there is power.
er for flood control and water
water for power....Power to g
Valley to a new generation Po
o make the river work!"
Pare Lorentz, l

few homes of the native mu

*T*he 31 jets of the Rivers *of Tennessee Fountains at Tennessee Bicentennial Mall State Park symbolize the state's major waterways and are framed by a curv-* *ing granite wall, engraved with quotes highlighting the water's importance. In addition to the history lesson, the fountains provide an ideal place to chill during the warm summer months.*

Nashville

*W*here there's smoke, there are bound to be members of the Nashville Fire Department working to contain it. More than 1,100 people comprise the department and fan the flames of its fire suppression, prevention, and education efforts.

*S*ailing on its twisting course through town, the Cumberland River—which brought the first European settlers to the area—helps keep Nashville's economy afloat, whether transporting goods or offering spectacular views of the city to sightseers.

Nashville

From its elevated location, the Eighth Avenue South Reservoir is a commanding landmark. Despite a rupture in 1912–loosing 25 million gallons of water that swept a number of homes from their foundations–the distinctive limestone structure has been in continuous use since it was completed in 1889.

*W*ater–it isn't just for bathing anymore. Wendy Kanter (ABOVE, ON RIGHT) is a licensed, Nashville-based practitioner of Watsu, a form of massage therapy conducted in a warm-water pool. At the Centennial Sportsplex Aquatics Center (OPPOSITE), the young and the young at heart can take advantage of recreation and competition pools, a diving well, and a full roster of fitness classes.

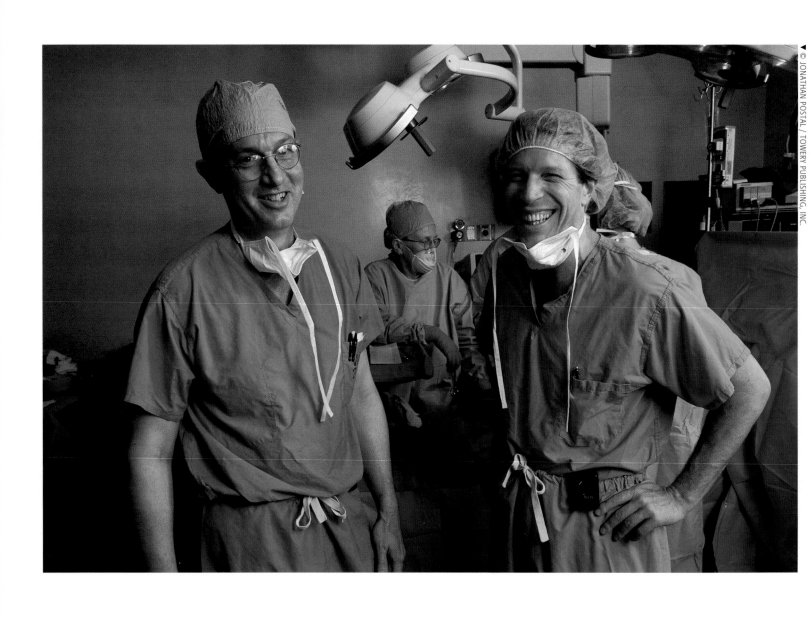

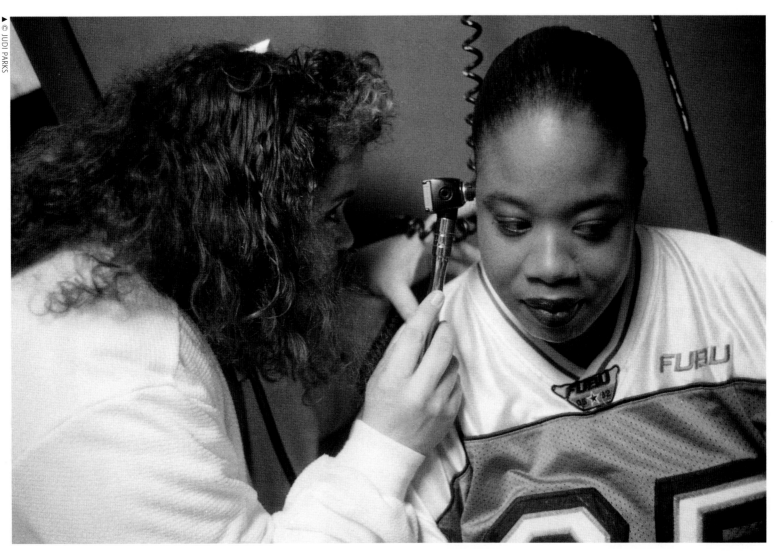

he health of all Nash-villians is a top priority for the city. At the Downtown Clinic for the Homeless (ABOVE), dozens of underprivileged patients each day receive free health care. The staff of Vanderbilt Medical Center, which became part of Vanderbilt University in 1874, includes notables such as (OPPOSITE, FROM LEFT) Dr. Noel Tulipan, director of the division of pediatric neurosurgery, and Dr. Joseph Bruner, director of fetal diagnosis and therapy.

CORNELIUS VANDERBILT.
BORN, MAY 27, 1794.
FOUNDED VANDERBILT UNIVERSITY MCH. 17, 1873.
DIED JAN. 4, 1877.

E very time the Vanderbilt Commodores take to the football field, they pay tribute to the school's founder, Commodore Cornelius Vanderbilt (OPPOSITE), who in 1873 endowed $1 million to what would become one of the top 25 uni- versities in the nation. Attended by some 10,000 undergraduate and gradu- ate students per year, the institution employs more than 12,000 faculty and staff members, making Vanderbilt the largest private employer in the region.

ince 1924, when it granted its first baccalaureate as the Agricultural and Industrial State Normal College, the school now known as Tennessee State University (TSU) has expanded in incremental degrees. TSU now offers its students more than 40 bachelor's and 20 master's programs, from African studies to accounting to architectural engineering.

Nashville

The oldest university in the city, Fisk University held its first classes in 1866, not long after slavery became illegal in the United States. When the university began suffering from its lack of funding in 1871, a group of students formed the Jubilee Singers (ABOVE) and traveled around the globe to raise money for their school. Today a thriving institution offering a liberal arts curriculum, Fisk offers joint degree programs with Vanderbilt University, Howard University, and Rush Medical Center.

Nashville

*B*elmont University, a liberal arts, Southern Bapist-affiliated school founded in 1951, harmonizes well with its setting at the head of Music Row. The campus' visual centerpiece is Belmont Mansion (OPPOSITE TOP), an 1853 house modeled after an Italian villa. Formerly the home of the wealthy Adelicia Hayes Acklen Cheatham, the mansion is open to the public for guided tours.

Nashville

*N*ashville's historic mansions—and the reenactors who now populate them during the day—stitch together a tangible guide to the area's rich heritage. The Federal-style Travellers Rest Plantation (ABOVE) *was built* by John Overton in 1799, and numerous additions were made to the farmhouse between 1808 and 1828. In its heyday, John Meade's Belle Meade Plantation (OPPOSITE) *was a worldfamous horse farm.*

he furor after the storm: Tornadoes devastated Nashville and the surrounding region in April 1998, causing nearly $100 million in property damage and an inestimable amount in personal loss. Some of the most well-publicized damage occurred on the grounds of the Hermitage (OPPOSITE), once the home of President Andrew "Old Hickory" *Jackson, where more than 1,200 trees—including the tallest tulip poplar in Tennessee—were toppled. Gibson Musical Instruments bought the lumber from that tree and used it to craft some 200 Les Paul Custom Old Hickory Guitars. Gibson's factory (PAGES 160 AND 161) has been part of the Nashville community since the 1970s.*

Nashville

Nashville

*D*uring the Battle of Franklin in November 1864, Carnton Plantation (ABOVE) *served as a field hospital, ministering to wounded Confederate soldiers. The house and grounds— including McGavock Confederate Cemetery, where thousands of soldiers were interred—are open for tours. The* nearby Lotz House Museum (OPPO-SITE), *built in 1858, houses the area's largest collection of Civil War artifacts on its first floor. Walking up to the second story, where the living quarters have been carefully preserved, visitors take a short trip back in time to the late 19th century.*

Nashville

O n November 30, 1864, the Civil War was brought forcibly home to the Nashville area when the Army of Tennessee attacked the Union stronghold in Franklin. One of the bloodiest skirmishes in the war, the five-hour Battle of Franklin–periodically reenacted–resulted in some 9,500 casualties, many felled by bullets that left their deadly imprint on a building at the Carter House.

Nashville

*T*hough grounded in the present and always looking toward the future, Nashville keeps evidence of its past alive as well. Set in stone and cast in bronze, memorials to soldiers of every era stand guard over the city.

Hills of Harmony

167

*W*nderlying the hush that enshrouds Mount Olivet Cemetery (ABOVE) and Nash-ville National Cemetery (OPPOSITE), hundreds of thousands of voices clamor for the chance to tell their stories. The 33,000 graves at Nashville National Cemetery, designated a U.S. military cemetery in 1867, include the resting places of nearly 13,000 Union Army soldiers. Those interred at Mount Olivet include civilians, Confederate Army officers, and soldiers who fought in World War I.

Nashville

Heeding the call: Nashville may still be part of the Bible Belt, but an ongoing influx of Muslims, Buddhists, and observers of other faiths has made the fabric of the city's religious tapestry infinitely more intricate.

*N*ashville's charitable spirit shines through during the holiday season as local organizations share the bounty with needy families. Everyone from Tennessee Titans Head Coach Jeff Fisher (OPPOSITE) to the U.S. Army gets in on the act of giving.

The carillon at Tulip Street United Methodist Church (RIGHT) has struck a chord with congregants since the late 1890s, when the 10 bells were purchased from the Tennessee Centennial and International Exposition. At the Eighth Avenue South Cokesbury bookstore's annual tent sale (OPPOSITE), inspirational reading issues a clarion call to bargain hunters. Cokesbury sells books put out by the Nashville-based United Methodist Publishing House and a wide variety of other publishers.

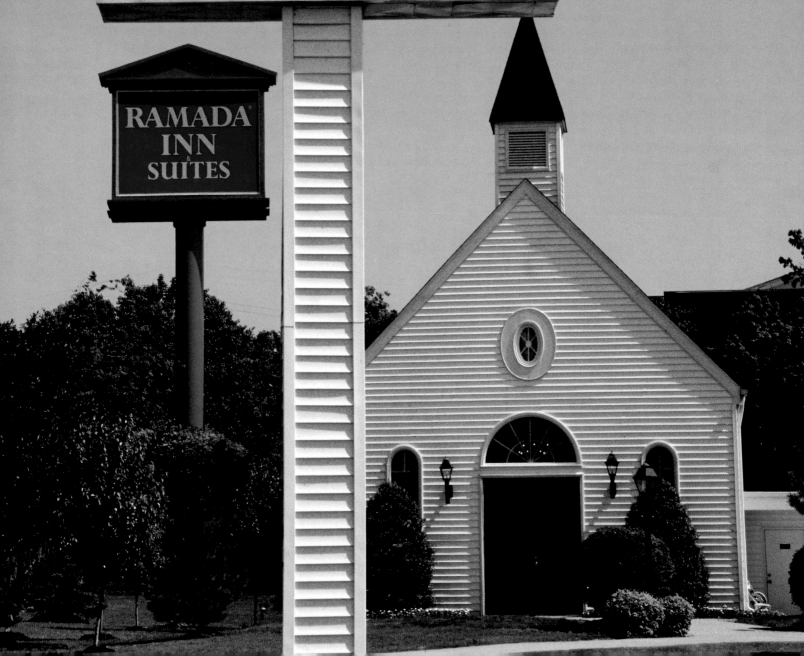

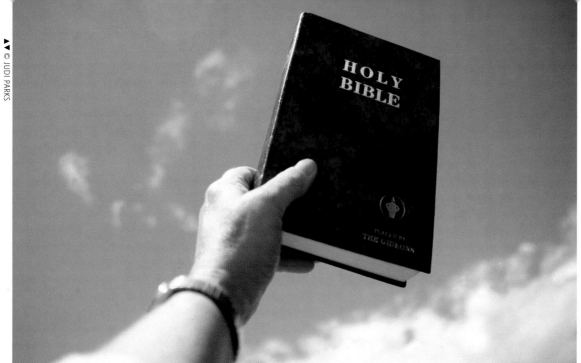

Since 1991, the rich, the famous, and the just plain folk have been turning to the Bridal Path Wedding Chapel as one site for tying the bonds of holy matrimony. As a result of the number of Music City celebrities who have married there, the Nashville fixture stands just this side of tourist attraction— and pretty close to a convenient honeymoon location, as well.

Nashville

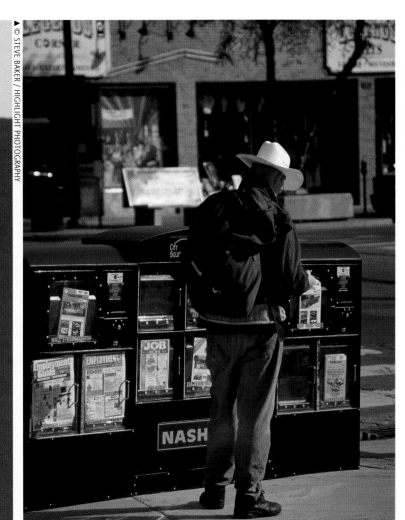

*F*aith and dreams are alive and well in the Nashville area, where the Ryman Auditorium, the Country Music Hall of Fame, and decades of musical innovation draw in droves of talented musicians hoping to break the sound barrier.

Hills of Harmony

Nashville

*R*ockabilly music comes alive in the original sounds of J.D. Wilkes (OPPOSITE) and his band, the Legendary Shack-Shakers. Songwriters everywhere can benefit from the protection offered by organizations such as ASCAP– the American Society of Composers, Authors and Publishers. Run by its members, ASCAP licenses and distributes royalties for public performances of copyrighted music for participating writers and publishers worldwide.

orch and twang: The smoky, electrifying jazz of vocalist Annie Sellick (RIGHT) and the rebellious, self-termed pulp country of Kristi Rose and Fats Kaplin (OPPOSITE) entrance their audiences and earn the singers ever growing numbers of fans.

*T*he flap over the Bluebird
Cafe has risen steadily since
the venue first opened in 1982.
Established primarily as a restaurant,
the Bluebird's reputation for great live
music quickly took wing, and the club
now has its own television show—
LIVE FROM THE BLUEBIRD CAFE—and
has been featured as the setting for
the film THE THING CALLED LOVE.

T here's some good eatin' at Rotier's Restaurant, owned and operated by the Rotier family since 1945. The food is simple—meat and three vegetables, cheeseburgers, and other standard fare—but the customers' lavish praise is the feather in the establishment's cap.

*I*n addition to a wide menu of great food, some of Nashville's restaurants serve up side orders of multitalented, creative folk. Vocalist Jenny Goforth (LEFT), selected as one of the musicians for the 2001 Country Music Marathon, also maintains a regular job at Rio Bravo Fresh Mex in the city's West End. At the Bound'ry Restaurant, owner Jay Pennington and Chef Theresa Everett (OPPOSITE, FROM LEFT) collaborate to produce perfect harmony between the eatery's upscale global cuisine and its lively atmosphere.

They said a mouthful: Purity Dairies isn't clowning around when it comes to quality. Founded in the 1920s as a small dairy, the company and its list of products have grown to brain-numbing proportions, covering everything from milk and ice cream to juice and bottled water.

Nashville

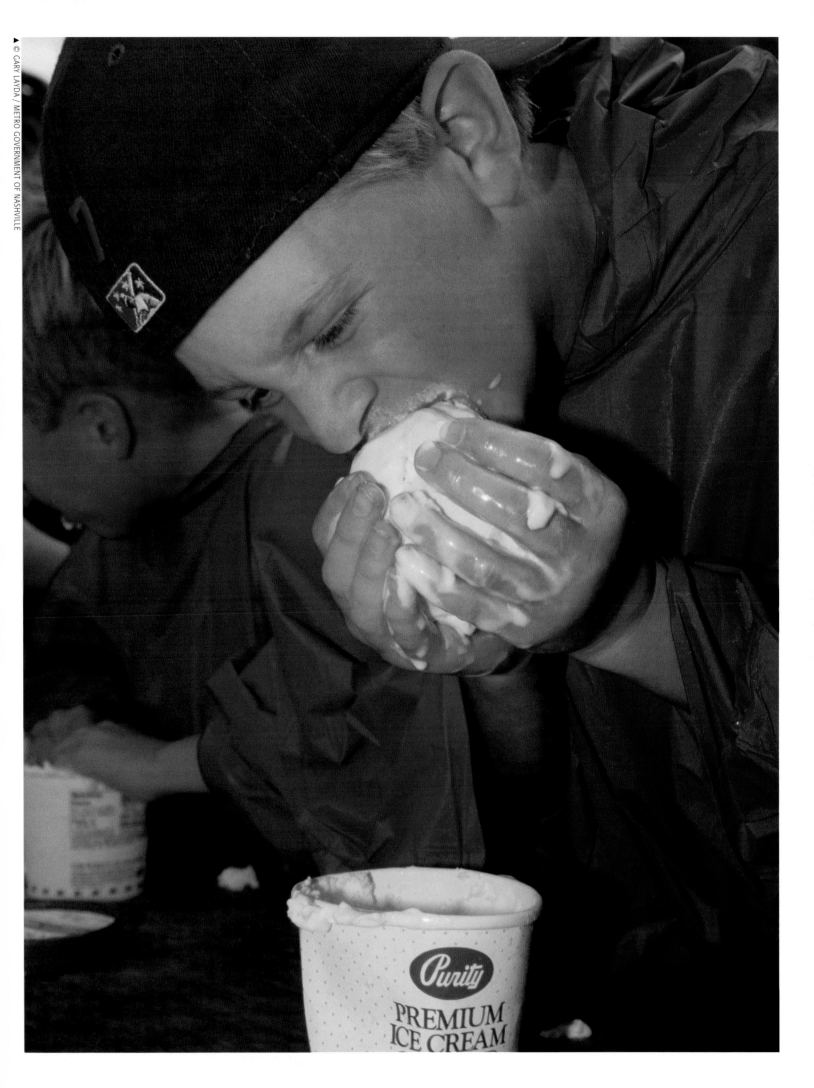

Purity
PREMIUM
ICE CREAM

As one of the country's 10 largest public electric utilities, Nashville Electric Service—NES—lights up the lives of more than 300,000 Middle Tennessee residents. Teaming up with the Cumberland Science Museum to teach kids about the powers and potential dangers of electricity, NES is one of the sponsors for the museum's ZAP exhibit (LEFT).

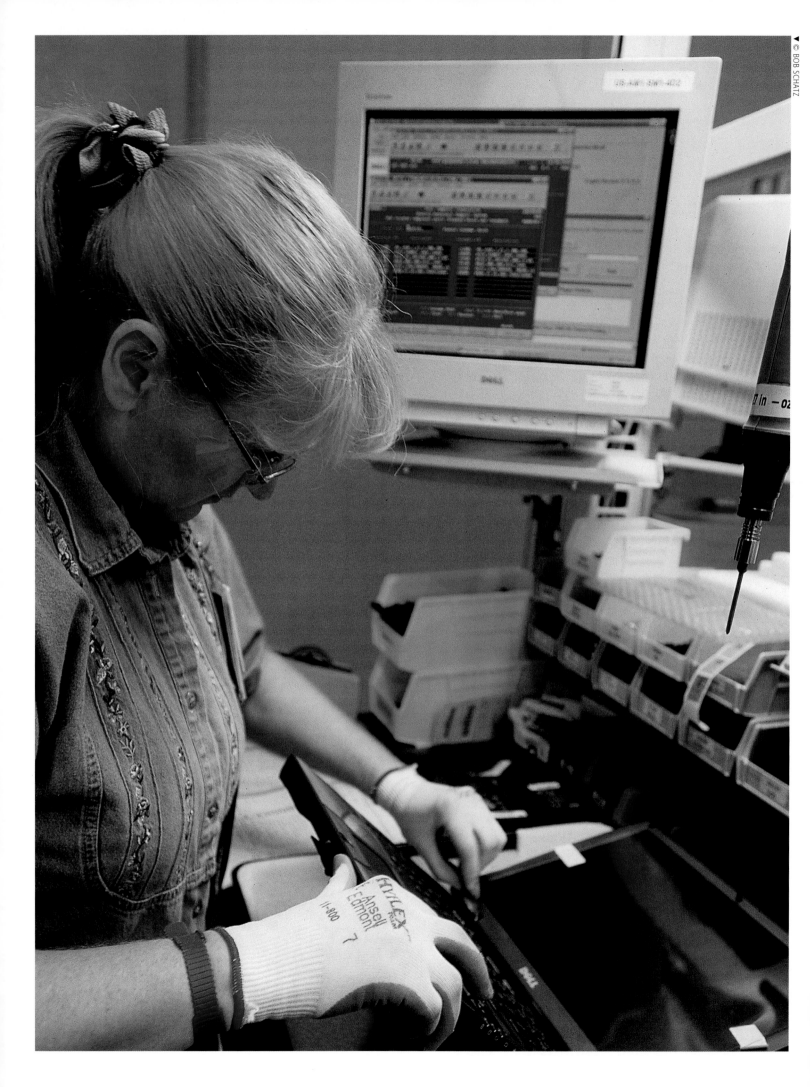

*H*igh-tech employment is on-line in Nashville, the site of one of Dell Computer Corporation's two U.S. manufacturing facilities. The plant—where Inspiron notebook computers are built—was constructed in Nashville in 2000 and has created some 3,500 jobs.

*N*issan Motor Manufacturing Corporation U.S.A.'s Smyrna site, located just southeast of Nashville, gives the regional economy a healthy jump start. The 5 million-square-foot assembly plant employs approximately 6,000 personnel to keep business rolling along.

*S*pirit by the carload looms large in Nashville, whether it's fueled by a burning passion for a favorite sports team, or just a well-oiled talent for monkeying around.

Nashville

*I*t's a jungle in here: The Nashville Zoo at Grassmere's Jungle Gym (LEFT) is a per- fectly acceptable spot for kids—up to 1,000 at a time, if necessary—to act like wild animals. At 66,000 square feet, the sprawling, volunteer-built playground is the largest of its kind in the world. The unusually friendly sea serpent at Fannie Mae Dees Park—also known as the Dragon Park (OPPOSITE)—adds more than 100 feet of climbing and playing space to its Vanderbilt-area neighborhood.

Nashville

At the Nashville Zoo at Grassmere, residents and visitors alike make the most of photo opportunities. The zoo, located on the grounds of historic Grassmere Farm, features animals—some housed in the Critter Encounters petting zoo—from four continents.

Nashville

egardless of the size of a patron's reading list, the Nashville Public Library system has it covered. The main library downtown and 20 branches throughout Davidson County are home to volumes of services, including a variety of children's programs.

Nashville

T hough it is best known as the home of country music, Nashville calls on a full range of voices—and all kinds of faces—to compose the rich harmonies that resonate across its hills (PAGES 206-209).

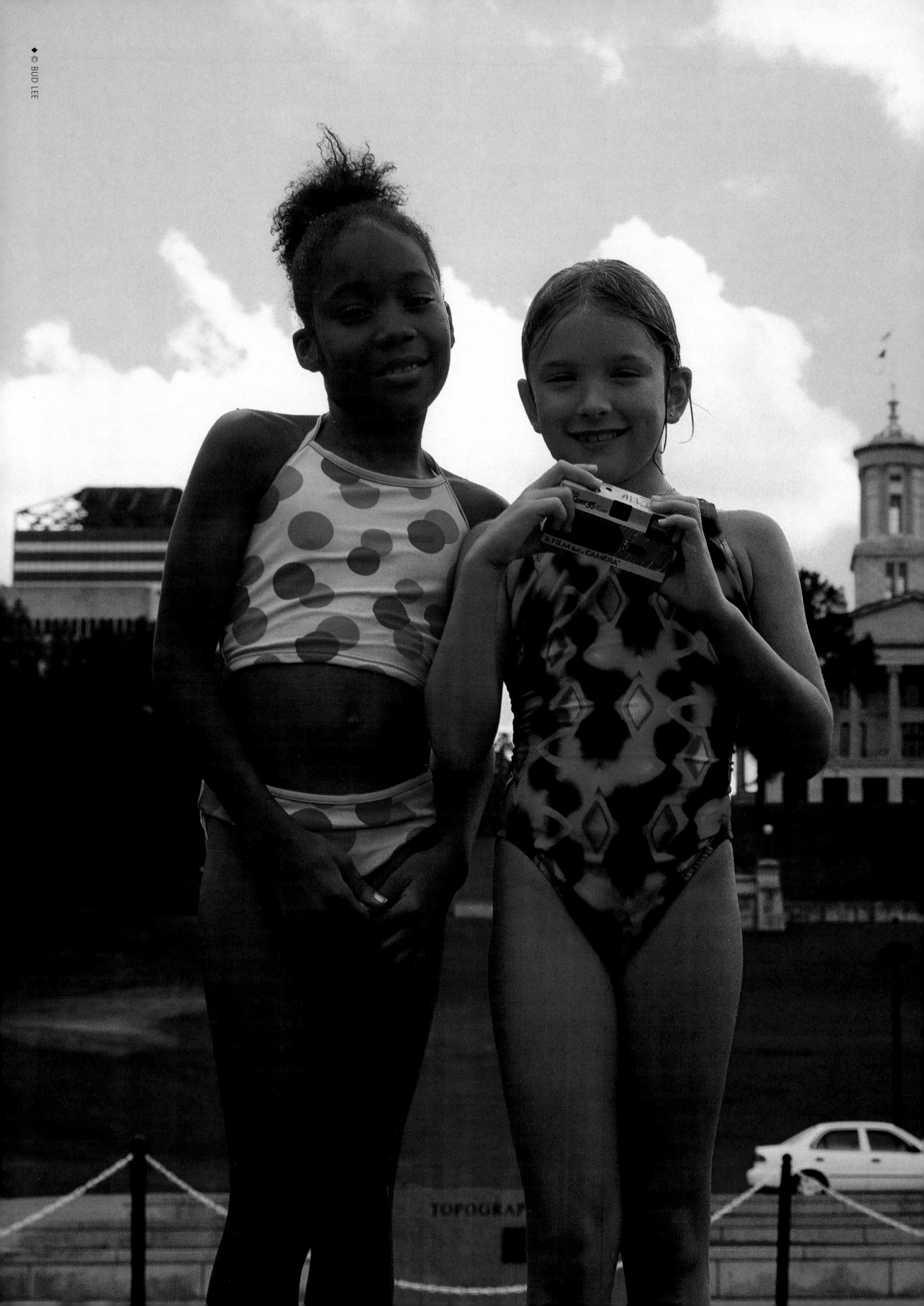

◆ © BUD LEE

Profiles in Excellence

A look at the corporations, businesses, professional groups, and community service organizations that have made this book possible. Their stories–offering an informal chronicle of the local business community–are arranged according to the date they were established in the Nashville area.

AIRPORT RAMADA INN & SUITES

AMSOUTH BANK

ANDERSEN

APAC-TENNESSEE, INC.

APEX & ROBERT E. LEE MOVING & STORAGE COMPANY, INC.

AQUINAS COLLEGE

BAPTIST HOSPITAL

BATTLE GROUND ACADEMY

BELLSOUTH TELECOMMUNICATIONS, INC.

CENTEX HOMES

CITADEL COMMUNICATIONS CORPORATION

COMDATA CORPORATION

COMMUNITY HEALTH SYSTEMS, INC.

THE CROMWELL GROUP, INC.

CRT, CUSTOM PRODUCTS, INC.

CURB RECORDS INC.

DOUBLETREE HOTEL NASHVILLE

HARDAWAY CONSTRUCTION CORPORATION

HARPETH HALL SCHOOL

HART FREELAND ROBERTS, INC.

HCA/TRISTAR HEALTH SYSTEM

LOEWS VANDERBILT HOTEL

NASHVILLE AREA CHAMBER OF COMMERCE

NASHVILLE BUSINESS JOURNAL

NASHVILLE ELECTRIC SERVICE

RENAISSANCE NASHVILLE HOTEL

SAINT THOMAS HEALTH SERVICES

SHERATON MUSIC CITY HOTEL

SOUTHWEST AIRLINES

TENNESSEE DEPARTMENT OF ENVIRONMENT AND CONSERVATION

UNION PLANTERS BANK

VANDERBILT PROPERTIES

VOLUNTEER STATE COMMUNITY COLLEGE

XO COMMUNICATIONS, INC.

YMCA OF MIDDLE TENNESSEE

Profiles in Excellence

1847	Nashville Area Chamber of Commerce
1875	YMCA of Middle Tennessee
1883	AmSouth Bank
1889	Battle Ground Academy
1898	Saint Thomas Health Services
1910	Hart Freeland Roberts, Inc.
1918	Baptist Hospital
1924	Hardaway Construction Corporation
1939	Nashville Electric Service
1946	Apex & Robert E. Lee Moving & Storage Company, Inc.
1948	APAC-Tennessee, Inc.
1951	Harpeth Hall School
1961	Aquinas College
1968	HCA/TriStar Health System
1969	Comdata Corporation
1971	Volunteer State Community College
1976	Andersen
1978	Vanderbilt Properties
1979	CRT, Custom Products, Inc.
1979	Doubletree Hotel Nashville

Nashville Area Chamber of Commerce

*I*n 1847, the sounds of Nashville's commerce included horse-drawn wagons on the bricks of Market Street, the ping of a blacksmith's hammer, the staccato precision of the *Republican Banner*'s printing press, and the gentle sounds of keelboats cutting through the Cumberland River. It was in that year that the Nashville Area Chamber of Commerce formed the organization that today

conducts the Music City's medley of thriving industries and economic growth.

With a macroscopic view of the future of Nashville, the chamber creates an array of programs to fine-tune business and livability quotients and ensure an attractive quality of life. Under the direction of a board of governors that is comprised of high-profile business leaders from the community, the chamber has spearheaded relocation efforts for professional sports teams, programs to bolster the vitality of downtown, improvements in education, technology programs, and efforts to ensure quality growth for the future.

The Nashville Convention & Visitor's Bureau, working under the guidance of the chamber, strives to communicate the area's distinctive historical and entertainment features, and to promote the city's convention and meeting facilities to a national and international audience.

GETTING DOWN TO BUSINESS

*W*ith more than 4,000 member companies, the Nashville Area Chamber of Commerce basks in a groundswell of membership participation. Chanting its "return on investment" mantra, the chamber challenges its members to invest time in its initiatives, which benefit Nashville's business economy and quality of life.

A stellar example of the chamber's initiatives is PARTNERSHIP 2010, established in 1990. Dedicated to the area's economic development, the program focuses on such factors as air transportation, automotive distribution, education, technology, quality of workforce, and workforce development—all which are critical in keeping Nashville competitive with, and marketable to, the rest of the world.

While working to strengthen existing business, PARTNERSHIP 2010 also strives to attract new business. Since its creation in 1990, PARTNERSHIP 2010 has played a part in bringing nearly 120 new or expanding companies to Davidson County, including such companies as Dell Computer, Sprint PCS, ADSC, and others.

Music City is frequently ranked as a hot spot for entrepreneurial and small-business activity. In fact, 92 percent of the chamber's membership is made up of companies with fewer than 100 employees, and 62 percent of the chamber's members employ fewer than 10 people. The chamber's

The Nashville Area Chamber of Commerce has worked as an advocate for local business since 1847.

Dell Computer Corporation is one of the Nashville area's success stories (left). The Wildhorse Saloon is a favorite nightspot among Nashville residents and visitors (right).

Small Business Council is dedicated to the growth and prosperity of these small businesses. For example, the Small Business Council coordinates Music City Future 50, which spotlights the fastest-growing privately held companies in Middle Tennessee; and FastTrac, which offers entrepreneurial training programs for start-up and existing businesses.

Nashville's downtown has enjoyed a renaissance in recent years, and the Nashville Downtown Partnership, created by the chamber as an affiliate in 1994, strives to ensure that the area remains a clean, vibrant, and safe center. More than 100 businesses in the downtown area have joined the Nashville Downtown Partnership.

The chamber views technology as a growing industry in the Nashville area, and brought the Technology Council on board in 1999, which now has more than 220 members, including local residents such as Dell Computer, Sprint PCS, and many more. The chamber also works to support and enhance Nashville's well-deserved reputation as the music/entertainment and health care capital of the country. The Nashville Health Care Council–a chamber affiliate–has more than 100 members, including health organizations such as HCA, Vanderbilt Medical Center, Renal Care Group, Inc., and many others.

QUALITY OF LIFE

Leisure activities, education, and the cost of living are equally important in shaping the area's overall quality of life. The chamber's Sports Council works to attract amateur and professional athletic events and provide recreational activities for area residents. The coun-

COUNTRY MUSIC HALL OF FAME AND MUSEUM
NASHVILLE

cil played a major role in the city's acquisition of the NFL's Houston Oilers–now the Tennessee Titans–an effort that captured the attention of numerous sports fans, as well as helping to bring about the arrival of the NHL's Nashville Predators.

The chamber is making its most important investment in tomorrow's leaders, having initiated an ambitious School to Career Program. The chamber's goal is–by the year 2010–for 100 percent of metropolitan students to successfully complete their high school education, thereby allowing them to make a successful transition from school to both career and further education.

Due to the tremendous growth of Nashville in the early 1990s, the chamber launched a Livability Index in 1995 that serves to measure and monitor quality-of-life progress and change. The index serves as an early warning system in the identification of any deterioration in quality-of-life attributes.

STRENGTHENING NASHVILLE FOR THE FUTURE

The chamber's focus on the future encompasses a number of key issues that are critical to the Nashville region's future success. Those issues include upgrad-

ing workforce availability and quality, improving the quality of the area's public education system, strengthening the region by improving the core city, and assessing the effect of rapidly changing electronic communication on businesses and lifestyles.

With a strong track record of getting in front of the issues, taking a stand, and articulating clear goals that generate results, the Nashville Area Chamber of Commerce will no doubt blaze a trail into the future, furthering its mission "to provide leadership that will help create the best possible place in which to operate a business while enhancing the Music City region as a desirable place to live, work, and visit."

Landmarks such as (clockwise from top left) the Country Music Hall of Fame, the Tennessee capitol, the Union Station hotel, and the Parthenon offer a variety of options for visitors and residents seeking education, entertainment, and fun.

With such musical outlets as the Bluebird Cafe and the Nashville Symphony, Nashville residents and visitors can always find a venue to satisfy their musical tastes.

YMCA of Middle Tennessee

Y MCA of Middle Tennessee has integrated itself thoroughly within the community and has established programs and services that have become a vital part of Greater Nashville. Founded in London in 1844 by a group of Christian men, the Young Men's Christian Association (YMCA) was first introduced to the United States in 1851, and to Nashville in 1855, with a stated objective

Clockwise from top:

The YMCA of Middle Tennessee has deep roots in Nashville. This postcard shows the YMCA building when it was located on 7th Avenue North in 1931.

The YMCA has always been a leader in water safety instruction, and teaches nearly 7,500 people how to swim each year.

The YMCA helps people grow in spirit, mind, and body by offering wellness programs and classes, providing financial assistance to those in need.

to improve the spiritual, mental, and social conditions of young men. Open to males under the age of 40 who were active in their churches, the association received initial interest in Nashville, but failed to survive the angst of the Civil War. In 1875, the chapter reorganized with 152 members. Perhaps no one at the time could realize how the YMCA's sphere of influence would increase throughout the years, adapting to the needs of each passing generation.

MORE THAN 125 YEARS OF SERVICE

The fledgling YMCA met in the rooms of the library association at the corner of Union and North Cherry Street (now Fourth Avenue North). In 1880, physical fitness became an important component of the YMCA's mission, and by 1912, the organization had moved into a new, eight-story

building on Seventh Avenue North, which included a dormitory, four gymnasiums, a swimming pool and club, and classrooms.

In the ensuing decades, the YMCA found itself assisting in war efforts. During World War I, the facility housed some 60 soldiers, and during World War II, an estimated 2 million men made use of the building.

The 1960s marked a banner decade for the YMCA. The East YMCA on Gallatin Road opened in 1962 and became the organization's first family facility. Another YMCA building was opened in 1969 on Hillsboro Circle, and is now known as the Green Hills Family YMCA. Also in 1969, the YMCA's hallmark Urban Services program, an inner-city outreach effort that serves at-risk youth, was launched.

Another growth spurt occurred in the 1990s as the YMCA opened nine new facilities. Today, there are 21 YMCA centers in seven counties across Middle Tennessee, as well as 345 program locations serving an average of 30,000 people per day. Membership has swelled to more than 100,000, with families comprising 71 percent of the membership. And to ensure

that everyone has the ability to participate, no one is turned away due to inability to pay. "One in four members is on some sort of financial assistance," says Ron Knox, chairman of the board of YMCA of Middle Tennessee.

BUILDING STRONG KIDS, FAMILIES, AND COMMUNITIES

The YMCA is a place where diverse groups find common ground in playing, learning, and working together," says Knox. "It creates opportunities for interaction that result in new friendships, new possibilities for personal growth, and a strengthened community."

The YMCA's comprehensive offerings include indoor and outdoor pools; steam, sauna, and whirlpool facilities; indoor tracks; racquetball and tennis

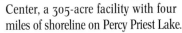

Center, a 305-acre facility with four miles of shoreline on Percy Priest Lake.

EMPLOYEES AND VOLUNTEERS

The YMCA employs some 3,100 staff members, who are supported by thousands of volunteers. Each YMCA is governed by a board of volunteers who strive to direct the organization's efforts in a way that is responsive to its specific community. Volunteers also serve as coaches for the YMCA's sports leagues, head fund-raising efforts, and are involved in tutoring and mentoring programs at the YMCA. In 2000 alone, more than 4,000 YMCA volunteers donated some 300,000 hours of service.

The tentacles of the YMCA of Middle Tennessee reach far beyond its members, though. With the mind-set that there doesn't need to be a facility to spread the organization's mission, the YMCA has partnered with more than 850 agencies, schools, and businesses to continue their work in building strong communities. In the years ahead, the YMCA wants to continue growing its sphere of influence in Middle Tennessee, serving more people and remaining responsive to the needs of the community.

The YMCA's Urban Services programs are an important part of the YMCA mission. The YMCA serves some 5,000 youth and reaches out to seven area housing projects. The YMCA also offers youth and teen programming that helps build leadership, teamwork, and character.

courts; wellness centers with weights and cardiovascular equipment; gymnasiums; group fitness classes; and a nursery with free child care.

"Our mission never changes, but our programs do, based on the needs of the community," says Knox. For example, in 1982, the YMCA introduced the Fun Company in direct response to the community's need for affordable, quality before- and after-school child care. The Fun Company now enrolls more than 6,000 children and works with 141 local schools.

In response to a greater need for a safe place for teenagers to go, the YMCA opened teen centers at six of its locations and a Teen Skate Park at three centers. The Cool Springs YMCA even offers a unique rock-climbing wall. And as today's senior population increases, the YMCA has initiated programs for active older adults, featuring water aerobics, special field trips, and luncheons.

Through the YMCA Urban Services and YMCA Community Action Project (Y-CAP) outreach programs, the organization encourages at-risk youth to grow up through the YMCA. "We are in a unique position to affect the lives of young people every day

as one of the largest youth services organizations in middle Tennessee," Knox says. Today, the YMCA offers free counseling and positive programs to almost 7,000 youth.

All children from an array of backgrounds benefit from the offerings at the YMCA. The organization promotes leadership opportunities through its Black Achievers, Leaders Clubs, and Youth in Government programs. Through its Youth Sports Leagues, the YMCA gives kids ages four to 17 the opportunity to learn teamwork and good sportsmanship, and as the nation's leader in swim safety, the YMCA taught more than 7,500 children how to swim in 2000. During the summer, kids can attend camp at the spectacular Joe C. Davis YMCA Outdoor

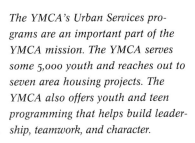

The YMCA encourages healthy lifestyles by offering group classes and counseling on everything from nutrition to spiritual healing.

AmSouth Bank

*A*mSouth Bank's focus has always been on the relationship–about people focusing on meeting the needs of people. That's what builds strong relationships. That's what builds success–with customers, with businesses, and with the Nashville community. ◆ AmSouth Bank in Middle Tennessee is the combination of two great financial

institutions–First American National Bank–based in Nashville and dating back to 1883–and AmSouth Bank–based in Birmingham with its origin in 1873. Both organizations were market leaders with a long history of caring about their customers and communities. Together, they create a premier financial services powerhouse with a huge presence and commitment in Nashville.

THE JEWEL IN THE CROWN

*N*ashville is AmSouth's jewel. It is here that the largest part of this $40 billion company is located. With more than 2,000 local employees, 80 branch banking offices and 300 ATMs, Nashville and Middle Tennessee are home to a significant investment in people and resources. A great deal of financial expertise is here, as AmSouth's Healthcare, Corporate Finance, Capital Markets, and International Banking divisions are all headquartered in Nashville.

As a result, AmSouth holds the

number one market share. More than $4 billion is held in AmSouth deposit accounts–representing a fourth of all of the dollars deposited in Middle Tennessee banks–and more than a third of all businesses–both large and small–in Middle Tennessee have a banking relationship with AmSouth.

AmSouth Bank's senior management team, branch managers, and key employees in Nashville are longtime, local bankers who know the market and its people well. With most having been in place since the mid-1980s, they have local decision-making power about loans, charitable contributions, and employee recruiting. On average, AmSouth hires one new employee in Nashville each day.

A BACKBONE OF NASHVILLE'S PROGRESS

*T*hroughout Nashville history, the bank has financed, influenced, or been involved in the critical economic development of the city and the region. From key chamber of commerce initiatives to charitable projects, professional sports to elementary education, AmSouth serves as a vital instrument in Nashville's progress.

In Partnership 2010, AmSouth is in a leadership role within a group of civic and business leaders in pursuing corporate headquarters, growing

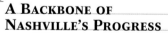

AmSouth Bank has more than 80 branches and 300 ATMs throughout Middle Tennessee.

80 works of art, including pieces from Picasso, Matisse, van Gogh, and Monet. AmSouth is a major sponsor of the Nashville Symphony, the Nashville Ballet, and the Nashville Opera. The company has been a longtime supporter of bringing the best of 42nd Street to downtown Nashville by sponsoring a variety of Broadway shows performed at the Tennessee Performing Arts Center.

AmSouth awards more than $1 million a year in contributions to nonprofit organizations in Nashville and Middle Tennessee. Employees serve in leadership positions in more than 150 nonprofit organizations such as schools, health and human service agencies, churches, arts, and cultural organizations.

HIGH TECH, HIGH TOUCH

*I*n keeping with the bank's focus on understanding needs, meeting needs, and building relationships, AmSouth offers a personal style of banking that is both high tech and high touch. A pioneer in the convenient 24-hour banking by phone, and an innovator in Internet banking products, AmSouth continues to keep the people they serve in mind.

It is much more than a financial institution. It's an organization of people living by an outstanding set of corporate values: "Do more than is expected. Improve someone's life. Make a difference. Make time for people. If something is wrong, make it right. And do the right thing."

In Nashville and Middle Tennessee, the people of AmSouth Bank make a commitment to customers to provide exceptional service and to the community to help make the city a better place to live and work.

AmSouth's focus has always been on meeting the needs of people.

existing businesses, fostering entrepreneurship, and protecting Nashville residents' quality of life.

AmSouth has committed to investing millions of dollars in affordable housing, low-interest loans and grants to families, small businesses, and nonprofit organizations. It is the largest local investor in the Nashville Housing Fund. AmSouth provides its expertise as well so new homeowners can be informed financially and legally, as employees educate low-income homebuyers in seminars held throughout the city on the buying process, investing, budgeting, and banking. AmSouth has also created a youth savings bank in a large north Nashville church to teach children how to use and save money.

The AmSouth Scholar program was created to award scholarships to students from low-income families to attend Fisk University and Tennessee State University. For students not yet in college, AmSouth supports the popular PENCIL program, a partnership between area schools and local businesses to make funds available to public schools and provide employees the opportunity to tutor students one-on-one.

In sports, AmSouth played a key role in bringing the NFL and the NHL to Nashville by its involvement in the recruitment and initial major sponsorships of the Tennessee Titans and the Nashville Predators.

AmSouth has long enjoyed significant partnerships with art, theater, dance, and musical venues, as well. The bank sponsored the inaugural exhibitions of the new Frist Center for the Visual Arts that brought more than

AmSouth has long enjoyed significant partnerships with art, theater, dance, and musical venues and organizations.

Battle Ground Academy

riginally built on the historic Civil War site of the Battle of Franklin, Battle Ground Academy (BGA) has served as a monument to education since its founding in 1889. Today, the independent, coeducational school has a student body of approximately 930 in prekindergarten through grade 12. ◆ In September 1889, BGA was opened on a six-acre

Battle Ground Academy's (BGA) history and heritage provide the cornerstone for all growth.

site purchased for $1,140 by W.D. Mooney and S.V. Wall with the help of local Franklin, Tennessee, citizens who contributed funds to build the school. In the early years, when it was customary to call a school by the name of its headmaster, the school was known as the Mooney and Wall School.

A STORIED PAST

BGA was disabled by a fire in 1902, forcing the students to move down the street and continue their course work at the Everbright mansion. The board of trust then bought 10 acres of property on Columbia Pike for $10,000 for the new school. September 1903 marked the completion of the new school building and the hiring of new headmasters, R.G. "Daddy" Peoples and J.H. Peoples.

Another fire struck BGA in 1910 and students again returned to the Everbright mansion. By September 1911, the new school building was complete, and it remains standing today. In 1925, a former BGA graduate, George Briggs, assumed the role of headmaster.

Also in 1925, two literary societies

were formed. The Greers took their name from former headmaster Greer Peoples, and the Platos were named after the Greek philosopher. At first, the societies were strictly literary, but eventually the activities broadened to include athletics. One of the primary purposes in founding the two societies was to develop in students a sense of fair play and good sportsmanship. These two societies are still a part of BGA today, as all students are either Greers or Platos.

While BGA had been coeducational since its founding, in 1929 it became an all-male school and remained so until 1979. Through the years, several headmasters have left their marks on the school, including Jonas Coverdale, J.B. Akin, and John Bragg. In 1990, Dr. Ronald Griffeth took the helm and, since then, the school has experienced

phenomenal growth. The Upper School moved to brand-new facilities on Ernest Rice Lane, the Middle School grew to incorporate fifth and sixth grades, and, in 1998, BGA acquired Harpeth Academy of Franklin, renaming it BGA Lower School.

COLLEGE PREPARATORY SCHOOL

We are a traditional college preparatory school," says Griffeth. "We focus on the basics." The basics are actually rigorous studies in foreign language, math, English, literature, history, and fine arts. A number of advanced placement classes are offered as well. BGA also places a high level of importance on communication skills, both written and oral.

Advances in technology are evident in all BGA classrooms. Computers are available in all Upper School and Middle School classrooms. Computer labs and instruction in usage are also available. More and more large-screen televisions that are computer compatible are being placed in classrooms for instructional use. The school also has a technology staff member who is specifically charged with helping teachers use technology and computers in the classroom, as well as with finding ways to make the computers most advantageous to students.

While technology plays an increasingly important role in students' learning, the heart of BGA is its faculty. "We have outstanding stability in our faculty," says Griffeth. "A number of the 90 members on staff have been here from 25 to 35 years."

Rounding out the college preparatory experience is a range of extracurricular activities that allows students to find a niche and develop a talent. Says Griffeth, "BGA offers

The campus-like atmosphere of the Upper School at BGA provides excellent facilities and space for learning.

Student life at BGA is enhanced by a wide variety of athletics and extracurricular activities.

all types of athletics for boys and girls. We also have an outstanding forensics program in which we often send two to five students to the nationals. Our theater program is expanding, offering more plays and musicals. Students can also hone their leadership and participatory skills in service clubs such as Key Club, Student Council, and Service Club, an organization which encourages students to volunteer in the school and community."

POINTS OF DISTINCTION

riffeth notes three points of distinction for the BGA student: "Our students embrace a great work ethic and feeling of responsibility that is exhibited in what they do inside the classroom and in their extracurricular activities. Development of character is important at BGA, and we make deliberate attempts to reward good character and punish mistakes.

BGA students, grades kindergarten through 12, enjoy pleasant surroundings and facilities.

And, finally, BGA prepares its students well for academics in college. Even if they don't do well gradewise here, they tend to do well in college." From a recent graduating class of 90, students have gone on to more than 40 colleges and universities. "This is important," says Griffeth. "This means that our

college advisers are working together with the students and finding colleges that match students' desires."

As for BGA's future, in an effort to consolidate the campuses, the historic Middle School campus has been sold to Williamson County and will move to the Upper School site when construction is completed. The construction is also incorporating a new Fine Arts Center that will house a new theater. The Lower School campus will eventually move nearer the main campus, once a new site is selected and purchased.

BGA plans to keep its student body size at a maximum of 1,000, believing that size has something to do with the culture or ethos of the school. Moreover, BGA's commitment to excellence and traditional values has made the school what it is today, and will sustain it for the next century and beyond.

BGA graduates attend selective colleges and universities across the country.

Saint Thomas Health Services

A dream became a reality for Bishop Thomas Sebastian Byrne and the Daughters of Charity of Saint Vincent de Paul when Saint Thomas Hospital opened on April 11, 1898. Now known as Saint Thomas Health Services, this nationally recognized institution has the distinction of being the oldest–and most successful–continuing operation in Nashville founded and owned by women.

Byrne, the fifth Catholic bishop of Nashville, wanted to establish a Catholic hospital in town since the only other Catholic hospital in Tennessee was located in Memphis. Nashville itself had 10 hospitals in 1898, including City Hospital, Hospital for the Insane, County Pest House, the newly opened Vanderbilt Dental Infirmary, and six smaller infirmaries. Byrne contacted the Daughters of Charity of Saint Vincent de Paul in Maryland–a Catholic community whose calling is health care and whose origins date back to 1633 in Paris, France–to determine if they would be willing to start a hospital in the city. Byrne also sought to obtain the mansion and eight acres of land owned by Judge Jacob McGavock Dickinson.

The Daughters of Charity eagerly accepted the challenge and, on January 6, 1898, the deed to the Dickinson estate was purchased. The next day, the *Nashville American* proclaimed, "Nashville's first great gift from the New Year will be a magnificent modern infirmary costing $150,000." It was decided that the hospital would be named for Byrne's patron saint, Thomas the Apostle. Sister Philomena Coupe was selected to take charge of the new hospital, which housed 26 beds in a total of 16 rooms, including a kitchen, a chapel, and living quarters for five sisters.

Within a few short years, the mansion-turned-hospital had become restrictive; new developments in medicine required more equipment, and an isolation area was needed for contagious diseases such as typhoid and tuberculosis. With support from local citizens and area physicians, funds were gathered to build a new hospital. Ground was broken on April 16, 1900, with the official opening on January 29, 1902. The new hospital would accommodate 150 patients, with rates beginning at $1 a day for a ward bed. The former mansion was converted into the Saint Thomas School of Nursing in order to provide a trained nursing staff for the new hospital.

In 1915, a $500,000 addition was made to the building at the intersection of today's Hayes Street and 21st Avenue. Decades later, the need for a larger facility became apparent, and construction began in 1972 on the current Harding Road site. The modern hospital opened in 1974, and in 1996, the name was officially changed to Saint Thomas Health Services. Today, the 571-bed, acute care facility is situated on a 44-acre campus and employs approximately 3,500 people.

More than a century has passed since its inception, but Saint Thomas' mission to carry out a healing ministry has remained unchanged. Saint Thomas is dedicated to providing

Founded by the Daughters of Charity in 1898, Saint Thomas Health Services is a member of Ascension Health, the nation's largest not-for-profit Catholic health care organization. The 571-bed hospital is located on the west end of the city and has undergone many expansions since it opened in December 1974.

This architectural rendering depicts the lobby of the Institute for the Healing Arts, which is scheduled to open in early 2002. The institute partners Saint Thomas with the YMCA to improve community health through education and prevention.

health services that are spiritually centered, accessible, and affordable. As a reminder to all, the hospital's values are mounted on a wall on the main floor: Service of the Poor, Reverence, Integrity, Wisdom, Creativity, and Dedication.

THE TOTAL PATIENT

While most recognize us as a leading cardiology hospital in the United States, we are much more than that–a hospital with a soul," says Thomas E. Beeman, president and CEO. "We are a community of healers because we feel we have a ministry. We have a commitment to be the light for the community of Nashville. The Daughters of Charity carry out their life's work here, and are a special resource to the hospital and our patients.

"Spirituality is an important part of healing," Beeman continues. "We want our entire staff to bring a special spiritual perspective into the workplace. Together, we can heal body, mind, and spirit."

In keeping with its values statement, Saint Thomas aims to provide the highest level of health care services for a population of more than 2 million in middle Tennessee, northern Alabama, and southwestern Kentucky. The hospital helps the poor and underserved in its Charlotte Family Health Center, and deploys the Saint Thomas NeighborCare van–staffed with a nurse, nurse practitioner, and paramedic–to go out into the community and serve those who can't come into the hospital.

As the only hospital in Nashville with a hotel attached, Saint Thomas also serves the families of the infirm. As a convenience for family members who need to stay several nights near their loved ones, the Inn at St. Thomas and Seton Lodge offer accommodations at a very reasonable rate. Further, an

entire ethics staff and committee are there to assist families in need, and pastoral care is also available.

"We endeavor to respond to the needs of our families," adds Beeman. "The clinical staff will take care of the patient, but we want to treat the total patient, and that includes the family." The family waiting room is staffed 14 hours a day by employees who are sensitive to the needs of families. They take telephone calls and messages, and provide food, compassion, and other personal services.

The entire hospital campus is user friendly, featuring enclosed parking and skywalks that connect to the hospital. The parking garage is staffed to facilitate the arrival and departure of elderly patients and others in need.

In another effort to provide easier patient access to cardiac diagnostic and treatment services and physician offices, the Saint Thomas Heart Institute, an 80,000-square-foot building, opened in March 2001.

"In designing this new facility, our goal was to apply all we know about superior clinical care to create a campus easier to use by patients and their families," says Beeman. "By locating cardiac services within one building– with dedicated parking and easy drive-up access–we are physically enhancing what is continually recognized as one of the best cardiac service facilities in the United States."

Since the 1960s, physicians and surgeons at Saint Thomas have achieved many firsts in the field of cardiovascular science: the first coronary artery bypass in Tennessee (1968); the first coronary angioplasty in the Southeast (1979); the first heart transplant

Saint Thomas is dedicated to providing health services that are spiritually centered, accessible, and affordable. Founded in 1898, the hospital relocated to its current campus in 1974.

The Saint Thomas Heart Institute added an additional 80,000 square feet during 2000 to meet increasing demands for its services. The institute has been a leader in treating heart disease for almost five decades and is consistently ranked among the nation's top five cardiac care programs (left).

Cardiac rehabilitation patients enjoy a workout at the Phase III rehabilitation program. After successfully completing Phases I and II at the hospital, many heart patients continue in the program for years, gaining positive physical, spiritual, and social benefits (right).

Sister Janet Keim, a Daughter of Charity who is also a nurse practitioner, serves patients in the Charlotte Family Clinic. Opened in 1997, the neighborhood clinic serves the west Nashville community with a variety of programs in addition to health care. The clinic serves many elderly, poor, and immigrant patients.

in Tennessee (1985); the first trans-telephonic cardiac rehabilitation program in the United States (1990); and the first installation of the SJM Regent aortic valve in the United States (1999). The hospital can also boast the first brachytherapy program in middle Tennessee, as well as one of the largest and most developed heart failure clinics in the United States.

COMPREHENSIVE SERVICES

*W*hether employing digital mammography; 3-D visualization of anatomy; a Stealth image-guided surgery system; or echoplanar MRI, allowing rapid detection of stroke, Saint Thomas utilizes cutting-edge technology in all of its departments. Saint Thomas is also renowned for its Dan Rudy Cancer Center, Vascular Institute, and neurosurgical departments. The latter features a new facility for the aggressive management of lumbar laminectomy procedures that involve the removal of vertebrae to reach the spinal cord, and allows patients to return home the same day as the operation. The orthopedic department has a state-of-the-art Hand Center and employs metal-on-metal hip replacement technology.

Saint Thomas offers the full spectrum of primary care and specialty services, including diabetes care, emergency, medical imaging, neurosciences, oncology, ophthalmology, orthopedics, pulmonary, psychiatric, and surgical services.

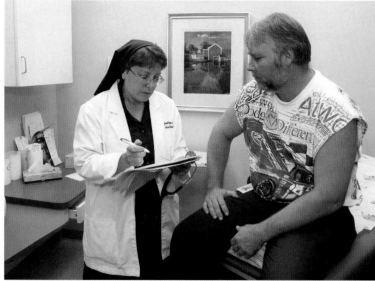

From a broader perspective, Saint Thomas remains committed to clinical research and education, providing a key part of the teaching program at Vanderbilt University's Medical School.

Saint Thomas' commitment extends to its staff as well. "We see investment in people as a great competitive advantage," says Beeman. In 2001, Saint Thomas embarked on a significant visionary leadership initiative. By 2002, some 500 staff leaders would have gone through a 12-week course that ultimately gives them the capacity to think differently about their work. In developing a significant learning organization, the hospital is taking a systems thinking approach to problem solving and developing transformational leaders.

Saint Thomas' leadership program is built upon the premise that leaders become diagnosticians–they are able to diagnose an organization's problems as readily as a physician can diagnose an illness. Equipped with the right tools, leaders are then able to recognize classic impediments to organizational growth.

A COMMUNITY RESOURCE

*S*aint Thomas strives to be an important community resource," says Beeman. "People have lots of demands on their resources. We want to participate in wellness, but don't want individuals to have to spend all of their resources on health care."

In 2001, Saint Thomas announced a landmark partnership with the

The NeighborCare Mobile Van takes primary care to many of Nashville's poorer communities, where lack of basic transportation prevents residents from staying well. The NeighborCare staff, including a nurse practitioner, assists with most health care needs and extends the Daughters of Charity's mission to serve the poor.

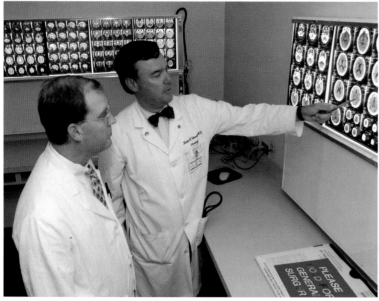

YMCA and its 21 Nashville-area locations. As health care partners, the two organizations aim to improve the community's lifestyle through education and prevention. For example, Saint Thomas will get involved in the Genesis program at the YMCA, which supports weight-loss goals, and the Restore program, which encourages people to regain the spiritual and mental confidence to start exercising. Through its unparalleled Lung Center, Saint Thomas anticipates that its partnership with the YMCA will help rehabilitate smokers.

Another entity that has far-reaching effects in the community is the Saint Thomas Foundation, which raises millions of dollars annually and supports charities, education, and research. The Saint Thomas Advocates, an employee volunteer program that began in 1995, provides help for numerous charities from Habitat for Humanity to United Way.

"We feel we are part of the community and encourage our employees to get involved in every aspect," notes Beeman. "If an employee sits on a community-based board, he or she can go to the foundation and ask for money for the charity. The foundation supports that. We don't just participate to be a good corporate citizen, but because it's the right thing to do."

Falling in the "right thing to do" category is the Welfare to Work program, which is run by women for women out of the hospital's Charlotte Family Health Center. This ongoing program takes 100 women who have no jobs or confidence in themselves and gives them the opportunity to learn job skills, as well as helping them to find jobs.

"We are not just a healing body, but a healing spirit," adds Beeman. "We want to help with community healing and need to be willing to walk on this journey together."

A SPIRITUALLY BASED HOSPITAL

*W*hile governed locally, Saint Thomas Health Services is part of Ascension Health, the nation's largest not-for-profit Catholic health system. Thus, the hospital has the financial strength to continue to reinvest in services and infrastructure. The hospital's support in these areas is apparent, as Saint Thomas' accolades have been constant through the years. Consistently rated among the nation's top five cardiac programs, Saint Thomas has also at various times been voted as one of the 100 top orthopedic hospitals in the country. Healthgrades.com has be-

stowed its only five-star rating on Saint Thomas for best outcomes in vascular and cardiology. In 2000, Saint Thomas was voted as one of the 100 best companies for working mothers by *Working Mother* magazine. Saint Thomas has also been named to *U.S. News & World Report*'s America's Best Hospitals list twice for excellence in cardiac care.

"We are on a mission," says Beeman. "We are focused on the future of medicine and on where we have the greatest strengths. And where we can't provide the service, we will collaborate to help others.

"The future is built on what we can imagine," Beeman continues. "We want to provide healing of mind, body, and spirit, as well as be effective stewards of a limited community resource—expenditures for health care. Ultimately, our goal is to be the premier spiritually based hospital."

The Saint Thomas Neurosciences Institute brings a unique depth of caring and clinical skill to the patient's bedside. Launched in 2000, the institute's health care professionals provide specialized care to help those with disorders and diseases affecting the brain, spine, and nervous system (left).

Nashville Mayor Bill Purcell congratulates Sister Priscilla Grimes, D.C., senior vice president of Mission Services, on the creation of the Nashville Consortium of Safety Net Providers. The consortium will serve nearly 50,000 citizens who have no health care insurance. Ascension Health, Saint Thomas' sponsor, has pledged continued funding beyond the first year of the program (right).

President and Chief Executive Officer Thomas E. Beeman assumed leadership of Saint Thomas in November 1999.

Hart Freeland Roberts, Inc.

*A*s Tennessee's oldest architectural and engineering firm, Hart Freeland Roberts, Inc. (HFR) has created a legacy of landmarks that shape the skyline of Nashville. From historic monuments such as the Parthenon in Centennial Park and the Ryman Auditorium to modern-day meccas like the Gaylord Entertainment Center and

From historic monuments such as the Parthenon in Centennial Park (bottom right) to modern-day meccas like the Gaylord Entertainment Center (top left), Hart Freeland Roberts, Inc.'s (HFR) designs have framed the history of Nashville.

Eugene Freeland and Martin Roberts, two of the founders of HFR, designed many of the bridges throughout Davidson County, notably the Old Hickory Bridge, which spans the Cumberland River (bottom left).

the downtown public library, HFR's designs have also framed the city's history.

TRACING ITS ROOTS

*H*FR traces its roots to 1910 when Russell Hart moved to Nashville from New York to design the Hermitage Hotel. Hart stayed in Nashville, seeing it as an ideal place to practice his own style of architecture. Simultaneously, Eugene Freeland and Martin Roberts, both engineering graduates from Vanderbilt, formed their own practice, and together designed many of the bridges throughout Davidson County, notably the Old Hickory Bridge spanning the Cumberland River.

After forming a series of individual companies, the trio merged in 1920. Early projects such as the Baptist Sunday School Board's Frost Building, the Life & Casualty office building, and the Duck River Dam revealed their extensive talents. Hart's good fortune continued when he was asked to re-create Tennessee's 1897 Centennial Exposition exhibit, the famous Parthenon.

CONTINUING THE LEGACY

*O*ne of HFR's most exciting projects was the 1989 renovation and expansion of the historic Ryman Auditorium, home to the Grand Ole Opry from 1943 to 1974. "We are very proud of that project," says Jeff Holmes, president of HFR. "It was a challenge to add the museum and the new entry, since we were dealing with a historic landmark with a distinct image."

In 1993, HFR, along with HOK Sports Facilities Group, was selected as the winner in a design competition for Nashville's downtown arena. The ultramodern sports and entertainment facility, now the Gaylord Enter-

tainment Center, features a radio tower spiraling into the sky. The radio tower design was selected as the predominant feature on the arena because most people in the early years were first introduced to Nashville by WSM Radio and the Grand Ole Opry. The design further acknowledges the city's musical roots by positioning the arena so that its axis is centered on the front doors of the Ryman.

In 2001, HFR added yet another landmark to the Nashville landscape. With HFR serving as architect of record and working in collaboration with Robert A.M. Stern in New York, the downtown public library, a $50 million project, opened amid wide acclaim.

SHAPING THE FUTURE

*T*oday, HFR is structured to create growth opportunities for its employees. Offering a full range of architectural/engineering services, HFR provides expertise in markets including health care, education, corporate, and environmental and transportation engineering, and it has one of the largest survey divisions in Middle Tennessee.

With more than 100 employees, HFR continues to grow consistently. The company maintains additional

offices in Jackson, Tennessee, and Kansas City, Missouri. "While a good portion of our business is in Middle Tennessee, the rest is spread throughout the country," says Holmes.

GIVING TIME AND MONEY

*H*FR involves itself in charitable work that is relevant to its employees and industry. HFR's employees give time and money to organizations ranging from Habitat for Humanity to the Red Cross and the American Cancer Society. The company has established a shadowing program, inviting high school students to learn and work in various capacities in the firm. HFR also created a scholarship in memory of one of its partners to provide assistance to students wanting to attend architectural school.

Hart Freeland Roberts, Inc.'s attention to detail and its client-focused mentality have led to numerous monumental projects that have become part of Nashville's architectural heritage. "Our history is our strength," says Holmes. "We've grown up with Nashville, and we've helped the region grow." More than anything, HFR has left a unique and lasting imprint on the city.

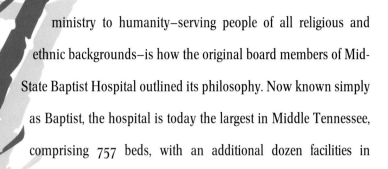

A ministry to humanity—serving people of all religious and ethnic backgrounds—is how the original board members of Mid-State Baptist Hospital outlined its philosophy. Now known simply as Baptist, the hospital is today the largest in Middle Tennessee, comprising 757 beds, with an additional dozen facilities in

Davidson and surrounding counties.

Baptist houses the largest and most comprehensive women's services and has the busiest emergency room in the city. The hospital also ranks as a leader in orthopedics and sports medicine, providing care for the Tennessee Titans and Nashville Predators. Through its efforts, Baptist has earned the privilege of being the first choice for care in Davidson County.

Baptist's history dates back to 1918 when Nashville's growth—coupled with the breakout of the influenza epidemic—initiated the founding of the original Protestant Hospital. In its first year, the hospital served 2,233 patients. However, 30 years later, Protestant Hospital was seriously in debt, having difficulty meeting the challenges of the post-war era. In

1948, the Tennessee Baptist Convention assumed ownership, and the hospital name was changed to Mid-State Baptist Hospital.

THE NEW HEALING HOSPITAL

Erie Chapman, president and CEO, notes, "Our Christian heritage is important to us." That heritage translates into what Chapman espouses as the new healing hospital, which is the "expression of Christian teachings about love and caring."

Baptist is creating a revolution from the inside, determined to establish an environment that is better than the typical American hospital. All 4,000 of the hospital employee partners and physicians are going through a re-orientation. "The new healing hospital is about creating the best possible experience for patients, families, each other, and ourselves," says Chapman.

"Since our work is sacred, our language reflects love. Our employees recognize that patients aren't broken automobiles but vulnerable human beings who need loving care as well as surgery or medicine," adds Chapman. "For the past two-and-a-half years, our leaders have undergone additional training with a goal

of being better at taking care of the people who take care of people."

For example, Baptist is making a concerted effort to improve the hospital experience for senior citizens. Free valet parking at a single, all-purpose entrance is now available for seniors. Volunteer chaperones greet them at the door. Once admitted, each senior is assigned a continuous care partner, who is on call as needed 24 hours a day.

A CARING COMMUNITY

"We are making real progress," says Chapman. Patient satisfaction scores support his comment. In a 1998 survey conducted by a national health care consulting firm, Baptist scored in the 68th percentile in customer satisfaction compared with 600 hospitals nationwide. In 2001, the marks increased substantially with a 99 percent rating for hospitals of comparative size and 95 percent for all hospitals.

Also in 2001, Baptist announced a partnership with Saint Thomas Health Services, another faith-based hospital in Nashville, in which the two will offer care under a unified organization. In the end, Chapman wants Baptist to be that caring community devoted to healing its patients with love in the Christian tradition.

Baptist Hospital is creating a revolution from the inside, determined to establish an environment that is better than the typical American hospital.

Hardaway Construction Corporation

*A*fter a tornado swept through the heart of downtown Nashville in the spring of 1998, the city stood in shock, witnessing the destruction of some of its beloved buildings, trees, and homes. In fewer than 24 hours, crews from Hardaway Construction Corporation arrived at the scene–unsolicited–and mobilized the company's

heavy equipment to begin removing the debris left in the wake of the tornado.

The dedication, teamwork, and commitment exhibited by Hardaway Construction in this unfortunate instance are at the heart of the company, a family-owned enterprise that has become one of the most respected and successful full-service construction firms in the Southeast. Centerpiece projects such as the renowned Opryland Hotel, the Tennessee Bicentennial Mall, and the Nashville International Airport expansion have cemented Hardaway Construction's reputation and serve to illustrate the company's diversification.

Hardaway Construction's history dates back to 1924, when 18-year-old L.H. Hardaway Sr. applied for a business license as a home builder. Since the legal age for obtaining such a license was 21, Hardaway had to make an appeal in court. He was granted his license and began building homes through the 1940s–many in the Edgefield/Inglewood area, where the company's current headquarters is located. When his son, L.H. Hardaway Jr., graduated from Vanderbilt and joined the business

in the 1950s, Hardaway began to place more emphasis on commercial and institutional construction. L.H. Hardaway Jr. now serves as the company's chairman, and his son Stan Hardaway, who joined the firm in 1985, serves as president and strives to carry on the company's strong family tradition.

Currently, Hardaway Construction achieves annual revenues of approximately $155 million, is licensed in 16 states, and employs some 400 people in three offices, including Henderson, Kentucky; Nashville; and Knoxville. Stan Hardaway notes that the company's hallmarks are its long history, its diversification, and the fact that, unlike other firms, it owns the heavy equipment used for its projects and still prefers to self-perform 25 to 30 percent of the scope of a project.

"We have been successful through the years because we try to monitor national programs and trends in the construction industry, and be the first to bring them to Nashville," says Stan Hardaway. "Ultimately, our success is due to our commitment to providing top-level customer service and competitive prices without sacrificing integrity and quality."

BUILDING HISTORY

*O*n a casual drive through Nashville, one is almost certain to see one or more of the many Hardaway projects–from modest to mammoth in scope–such as the Willis Corroon headquarters (One Century Place), Riverfront Park, Sheraton Music City Hotel, Sony Music Office Building, Vanderbilt University Medical Center East, Baptist Medical Plaza Tower II, Belmont University's Massey Business Center, Opryland Springhouse Golf Club, Riverbend Maximum Security Prison, Richland Creek Apartments, U.S. Tobacco Plant & Distribution Center, Bluegrass Country Club, and First Baptist Church in Hendersonville.

No doubt, Hardaway's showcase is the Opryland Hotel, which first opened in 1977 and today is the largest hotel without a casino in the United States, touting 2,870 guest rooms and 300,000 square feet of exhibit space. As the only contractor to be at Opryland since its inception, Hardaway has been through all four major expansion phases for the hotel. The company served as the sole contractor for the magnificent Delta Expansion, which, at $152 million, was the largest

Hardaway Construction Corporation was founded in 1924 by L.H. Hardaway Sr. (left): The company is currently led by L.H. Hardaway Jr., chairman (center) and Stan Hardaway, president (right).

private project in Nashville construction history. The addition, which spans 4.5 acres, is completely under glass, and features a quarter-mile river with boats, restaurants, shops, and meeting rooms.

Hardaway can boast many firsts throughout the region. The company built Hubbard Hospital, the first high-rise hospital in the city, as well as Rivergate Mall, Nashville's first regional shopping mall. The firm also pioneered the conversion of an old warehouse building on historic Second Avenue into residential living quarters, and built the first downtown condominium/office building on Union Street.

Hardaway received a major award for building the Tennessee Bicentennial Mall, earning a national Construction Award of Excellence from the Associated Builders and Contractors for its work on the urban mall. Other projects receiving regional awards include Nashville International Airport improvement program, Middle Tennessee State University Library and Greek Row, Father Ryan High School, St. Cecilia Cemetery Walls and Walkways, Opryland's Cascades Lobby and Delta Expansion, Bicentennial Mall World War II Memorial, and Belmont University Leo Center for the Visual Arts.

A TEAM APPROACH

"Our people make us special," notes Hardaway. "They are educated, dedicated, well-trained, experienced professionals. Our employees work in groups that are client driven. The smaller groups afford clients the personal attention they deserve, as well as a number of operating efficiencies."

Philosophically, Hardaway Construction is committed to a team approach to construction, with the

owner, architect, and contractor all working together from the inception of the project. By offering preconstruction services to its clients, the company enables an end result in dollar savings, tighter scheduling, and optimum use of materials and methods.

Hardaway parlays its dedication to its clients and to its employees as well. The company is family oriented, instilling a trusting, secure, and friendly workplace environment. Hardaway provides additional professional training for its employees, as well as sponsoring a General Educational Development (GED) program for employees and subcontractors/vendors. With an increasing Hispanic workforce,

Hardaway offers English as a second language to employees and Spanish for English-speaking employees.

Hardaway Construction Corporation embraces a mission statement that fosters a team spirit and partnership among its employees, clients, and community. The firm's mission calls for providing a quality product within a client's budget, serving clients with integrity and honesty, and striving for continuous improvement in services to the client, in the working environment, and in benefits for employees. With that in mind, Hardaway aims for steady growth as the company continues to build the future of Nashville and Middle Tennessee.

Hardaway's most notable projects include (clockwise from top) the expansion at Opryland Hotel, the Willis Corroon office building, and the addition to the First Baptist Church in Hendersonville.

Nashville Electric Service

As one of the 12 largest public electric utilities in the nation, Nashville Electric Service (NES) supplies power to some 324,000 residential, business, and industrial customers in a service area that encompasses all of Davidson County and portions of six surrounding counties. NES boasts rates that are among the lowest in the nation, which helps to fuel the

bustling economy in the Middle Tennessee area.

Established in 1939, NES has a rich history and a deep commitment to Nashville. NES is a not-for-profit utility that is owned by its customers and governed by a five-member board. Board members, who serve without pay, are appointed by the mayor and confirmed by the city council. NES contributes significantly to the economic well-being of the community by providing quality electric service at the lowest possible cost and by making the largest tax payments—approximately $14 million annually—of any area company.

NES also serves the community through its ongoing safety and education programs that have been expanded to include the Hispanic population and senior citizens, as well as elementary and high school students. In addition, NES' employees are involved in the community on a personal level, working with charitable and civic organizations throughout the city on a wide range of projects and service programs.

Solar panels installed at the Cumberland Science Museum in Nashville provide renewable energy to Tennessee Valley residents. Customers who want to use renewable energy resources to improve the environment may purchase Green Power Switch® from Nashville Electric Service (NES), power generated by the sun, wind, or landfill gas.

PLANNING FOR THE FUTURE

Anticipating changes in the electric industry, NES is taking steps to prepare for an increasingly competitive environment. Improving customer service and reliability are two major undertakings for the utility. NES regularly uses focus groups, telephone and written surveys, and pilot programs to determine what customers want and to identify needs specific to certain customer groups.

Research shows that while service has become more reliable since 1996, customer perceptions and expectations have changed. Residential, small-business, and large commercial and industrial customers are increasingly dependent on electricity and expect more reliable power than ever before. A major reliability study conducted on behalf of NES suggested a comprehensive review of tree trimming and a replacement timetable for aging electrical equipment. The utility plans to allocate additional resources in both of these areas to improve overall reliability.

NES has already made many service improvements, including installing new telephone systems and computerized equipment to handle the large volume of phone calls received during outages and to allow for faster restoration following emergencies. In addition, policies have been changed to make it easier to do business with NES. These policies include allowing customers to sign up for service a number of ways rather than in person, accepting credit cards for payment of electric bills, and providing staff to answer customer questions 24 hours a day, seven days a week. And a program called the Power Promise guarantees that NES will perform certain business functions promptly and efficiently, such as turning service on or off, and providing accurate billing or the customer receives a credit.

For more than 60 years, Nashville Electric Service has been an excellent corporate citizen—committed to good financial stewardship and giving back to the community in tangible ways. NES looks forward to continuing its history of service to the community, and remains committed to its mission to provide reliable, safe, and economical electric power for the comfort, convenience, and security of its customers.

As one of the 12 largest public electric utilities in the nation, NES supplies power to some 324,000 residential, business, and industrial customers in a service area that encompasses all of Davidson County and portions of six surrounding counties.

When Fred Duke Sr. returned to Nashville following his service in World War II, his first job was to deliver coal and ice. On weekends, to make a few extra dollars, he helped people move. At a time when the van line industry was in its infancy, Duke literally made his move and, in 1946, turned his weekend venture into a full-time affair.

In 1964, Duke decided to sell this business. After an eight-year hiatus, he had a yearning to get back to business and purchased Robert E. Lee Moving & Storage, a Nashville-area mover founded in the 1920s. In 1978, Duke acquired Apex and merged the two to form Apex & Robert E. Lee Moving & Storage Company, Inc. At the time, the company was associated with Bekins Van Lines, but, in 1992, the company became affiliated with Mayflower Transit, which remains its affiliation today.

In 1986, a second generation of the Duke family took over Apex & Robert E. Lee, with the brother-and-sister team Mark Duke and Frieda Smith serving as co-owners. Mark Duke, who assumed management responsibilities when he was only 18, had grown up in the business. Those skills have served him well as he continues to expand the company's horizons and put money back into the firm to maintain state-of-the-art facilities, trucks, and equipment.

Under the siblings' leadership, Apex & Robert E. Lee has evolved into a major firm handling interstate and international moves. With 50 full-time employees, the company consistently stays in the top 25 of Mayflower's more than 450 agents nationally for sales and quality.

THE LONG HAUL

The bread-and-butter business for Apex & Robert E. Lee is in national and account-based moves. Holding contracts with numerous national corporations, the company handles all employee moves, whether local, intrastate, interstate, or international. The firm also manages these same moves for individuals.

Apex & Robert E. Lee also handles more office moves in Nashville than any of its competitors. The Nashville Chamber of Commerce, Country Music Hall of Fame, Ben West Library, Frist Visual Arts Center, and American General, among others, entrust their wares to the company. The firm also serves as a distribution center–receiving, storing, and moving much of Nashville's infrastructure. As office rents increase, permanent record storage has also become a growing part of Apex & Robert E. Lee's business.

FIRST-RATE FACILITIES

Command central for Apex & Robert E. Lee is the firm's 80,000-square-foot warehouse, which offers first-rate facilities and all of the equipment necessary for its variety of moves. Other movers even rent the company's equipment. Immaculately clean and orderly, the warehouse is stacked three high in vaults

holding people's treasured belongings, floor-to-ceiling racks for permanent record storage, and a distribution area for quick-turn jobs. Any goods coming in or out of the warehouse are carefully inventoried to help track all merchandise.

Apex & Robert E. Lee's sales and management teams also work from this facility, where they pride themselves on being a partner to the company's clients. The company backs up all employees from sales to operations with continued industry education.

With the transportation bill in the 1980s calling for deregulation of the industry, many movers went out of business. But with its strong operations, professional service, and excellent standards, Apex & Robert E. Lee Moving & Storage Company, Inc. thrived, and the company is flourishing today. Plans to open new markets are under way and are setting the stage for the future.

The Apex & Robert E. Lee Moving & Storage Company, Inc. sales and management teams pride themselves on being a partner to the company's clients.

From left:
Apex & Robert E. Lee handles more office moves in Nashville than any of its competitors.

Immaculately clean and orderly, Apex & Robert E. Lee's 80,000-square-foot warehouse offers first-rate facilities and all the equipment necessary for the company's variety of moves.

Apex & Robert E. Lee also serves as a distribution center–receiving, storing, and moving much of Nashville's infrastructure.

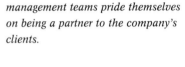

APAC-Tennessee, Inc.

For more than 50 years, APAC-Tennessee, Inc.'s Nashville division has worked in the private and public sectors, paving and resurfacing roads, as well as providing base operations for signature projects such as Opry Mills, Adelphia Coliseum, Gaylord Entertainment Center, and Cool Springs Mall. ◆ APAC is a wholly owned subsidiary of Kentucky-based Ashland, Inc., which

is one of the largest asphalt paving companies in the country, and which also owns Valvoline and Ashland Chemical. "While we have the financial backing and stability of a large company, we are locally managed and can provide the attention and service our customers need," says Mike Maynard, APAC-Tennessee division president. "All decisions are made here."

APAC's Nashville roots date back to 1948, when the Warren brothers–who had received the original patent for asphalt while working in Cambridge, Massachusetts–established operations in the city in the 1900s. The Warrens' work changed the face of transportation in the 20th century. The company became an integral part of paving the highways and roadways in the Nashville area; in 1968, the firm was purchased by Ashland, Inc. and renamed under the trade name APAC. Today, the company has some 250 employees, with branches in McMinnville and Crump, Tennessee, and asphalt plants in Nashville, McMinnville, Celina, Franklin, Parsons, and Crump, Tennessee.

APAC-Tennessee's Nashville division is one of four APAC divisions in Tennessee, and among 48 divisions in Alabama, Arkansas, Florida, Georgia, Kansas, Kentucky, Mississippi, Missouri, North Carolina, Oklahoma, South Carolina, Tennessee, Texas, and Virginia. The territory for APAC's Nashville division spans from 50 miles west of the Tennessee River to Cookeville in the east, and from the Kentucky state line in the north to the Alabama state line in the south.

SMOOTH OPERATOR

Base and pavement operations, as well as curb and gutter, are APAC's central areas of expertise. With more than half of its business in paving roads, the company's employees and equipment have worked, in part, on virtually every interstate and highway in the Middle Tennessee area. The company is the beneficiary of numerous smooth pavement awards given by the state.

A special niche for APAC is its big commercial projects such as Opry Mills and Adelphia Coliseum. "Our niche is working these large specialty projects that tend to require more management

and more thought process," says Maynard. "Our forte is the quality of our work. We get the big projects because of our quality and our ability to deliver on time." APAC also works on numerous government projects in its territory, including the taxiways and runways at the Nashville International Airport.

APAC works closely with engineers and architects to determine the best approach to a project, and offers innovative solutions and accurate production schedules. While providing quality roads and construction projects is APAC's goal, its number one priority has always been the safety of its employees. APAC can boast an accident rate that is among the lowest in the industry. Additionally, the company strives to protect the environment, provide clean air and water, and research new construction and recycling technologies.

Whether working on large, commercial projects or the city's roadways, APAC-Tennessee, Inc. continually offers competitive costs and inventive solutions for clients–as well as ensuring job safety for its employees–as it paves the way into the future.

For more than 50 years, APAC-Tennessee, Inc.'s Nashville division has worked in the private and public sectors, paving and resurfacing roads, as well as providing base operations for signature projects such as Opry Mills, Adelphia Coliseum, Gaylord Entertainment Center, and Cool Springs Mall.

H

arpeth Hall School, recognized as one of the finest independent schools for girls in the country, staged a yearlong celebration of its 50th anniversary in 2001. Founded in 1951 after the closing of the Ward-Belmont Preparatory School, Harpeth Hall began in one building with 161 students. Today, enrollment

stands at more than 550 girls on a campus that houses seven buildings, including a new, state-of-the-art library and information center that opened in the fall of 2001.

In 1951, Ward-Belmont–under financial duress–was shuttered and hastily sold to the Tennessee Baptist Convention, which moved its offices to the site. Hearing the news of the quick sale of their beloved school, a number of concerned parents and citizens of the community banded together to formulate plans for a new school. The group secured the former Estes estate, retained the headmistress and many teachers from Ward-Belmont, and miraculously opened the Harpeth Hall School that fall.

Buildings, athletic and fine arts facilities, and landscaping have been added to the 34-acre campus through the years in an effort to support the growing student body. Today, some 550 young women attend what is Nashville's only independent, all-girls college preparatory school. The heart of the campus remains the former Estes home, now known as Souby Hall, which houses administrative offices.

INSPIRING INTELLECT AND CREATIVITY

In its mission statement, Harpeth Hall "challenges each student to develop her highest intellectual abilities, to discover her creative talents, and to make a meaningful contribution to her community." Recognized as one of the foremost educational institutions in the nation for girls today, Harpeth Hall emphasizes a rigorous liberal arts curriculum, complemented by academic travel, a work-study program, and strong cocurricular programs.

Harpeth Hall's Winterim program provides opportunities for students

to learn and achieve outside the classroom in nontraditional areas. Also, the school offers more than 70 courses at the Upper School level, including numerous advanced placement classes. Three Presidential Scholars have been named from Harpeth Hall since 1990.

Harpeth Hall has been praised as an excellent model for integrating technology into the classroom. All of the school's teachers have laptops, and all students in grades seven through 12 own and use laptops. "It is particularly important in today's society for students to be well versed in technology," says Ann Teaff, head of Harpeth Hall since 1998. "No matter what career paths our students take, technology will play a key role, and it is our duty to provide them with the educational foundation they need to succeed in college and beyond."

EXPLORING THEIR POTENTIAL

Harpeth Hall students have ample opportunity to explore areas of interest beyond academic pursuits. The school boasts 12 varsity athletic teams, many of which have reached championship level in the city and state; an exceptional art program; and stellar dance, theater, and music programs, which

showcase young performers to the community in annual concerts.

Harpeth Hall is committed to community service, and 95 percent of the student body takes part in some type of service activity. Students also have opportunities to participate in a wide variety of on-campus organizations, academic clubs, honorary societies, civic organizations, language clubs, science clubs, and outdoor programs.

As Harpeth Hall looks to the next 50 years, it stands poised to continue building upon the foundation of educational excellence for women established in Nashville some 135 years ago.

Harpeth Hall students have ample opportunity to explore areas of interest beyond academic pursuits. Among the school's offerings are 12 varsity athletic teams, many of which have reached championship level in the city and state; an exceptional art program; and dance, theater, and music programs, which showcase young performers in annual concerts.

Aquinas College

Aquinas College, a small, coeducational, liberal arts college situated five miles from downtown Nashville, boasts significant benefits for its student body. Personal attention, small class sizes, convenience, little bureaucracy, and an easy-to-navigate campus with no-hassle parking are a few of the reasons why students attend Aquinas, a four-

Personal attention, small class size, convenience, little bureaucracy, and an easy-to-navigate campus with no-hassle parking are just a few of the reasons students choose Aquinas College.

year Catholic college founded in 1961 and administered by the Dominican Sisters of the St. Cecilia Congregation. "The value-added benefit is that we offer an ethical, Christian environment in which to learn," says Sister Mary Evelyn Potts, president of Aquinas.

Aquinas offers a welcoming and supportive environment for students who come from diverse economic, ethnic, and religious backgrounds. "We provide an affordable education that is the best deal in town for a private liberal arts college," adds Potts. "We have a student body of 600, including our PRIMETIME students, and an average class size of 15. Students love the ability to meet with individual professors and have them so accessible."

Because Aquinas is not a research university, the faculty emphasizes the students, not publishing research papers. All professors have full credentials, and no teaching assistants are used. Aquinas employs a number of adjunct professors who are practicing professionals, which allows students to stay abreast of current workplace trends.

ASPIRING TO ATTEND AQUINAS COLLEGE

Aquinas is heralded for its programs in nursing and teacher education. Through a partnership with Saint Thomas Hospital, the college's nursing students receive extensive clinical experience. The students' learning in a Christian environment, coupled with their knowledge of how to care for patients, contributes to the high recruitment rate of Aquinas graduates.

Aquinas' teaching tradition is equally strong. The college prepares students to teach in parochial, private, and public schools, and provides extensive student-teaching experience. Student Amy Lavender notes, "I came to Aquinas because the word on the street is that Aquinas College is the place to go for a degree in education."

Aquinas also offers a liberal arts degree and a bachelor of arts degree in business administration. The college's Web site, www.aquinas-tn.edu, details course offerings. Aquinas' practical and career-oriented curriculum permeates all academic programs, and con-

tributes to a high percentage of job placement for its graduates.

TRADITION AS EDUCATORS

Known internationally as great educators, the Dominican Order dates back 800 years. The Dominican Sisters came to Nashville in 1860 and became the Congregation of St. Cecilia. In 1928, the sisters joined with the Catholic University of America, beginning a normal school for the education of the sisters. In 1961, the normal school was replaced with Aquinas College, and moved from the St. Cecilia Motherhouse to its present location in west Nashville. St. Thomas Aquinas was named as the patron saint of the college.

In 1994, Aquinas was granted accreditation by the Southern Association of Colleges and Schools to award a bachelor of science degree in interdisciplinary studies (teacher education). Aquinas has continued to add baccalaureate offerings to complement the needs of its student population. The addition of weekend and evening

classes has further assisted the college's adult learners.

Aquinas' stately mansion, known as the White House, is used for business and administration, and dominates the entry into the 92-acre campus. The central academic building includes the Ann and Monroe Carell, Jr. Technology Education Center, which features state-of-the-art computers utilizing the latest in software and Internet technologies. The St. Dominic Education Center serves as the faculty office building for the education faculty. As a commuter college, students are assisted with off-campus housing.

ACCELERATING WITH PRIMETIME

*S*eptember 2000 marked a dramatic turn for Aquinas. The college launched PRIMETIME, an accelerated, nontraditional program designed to enable working adults to finish their degree in a timely manner without sacrificing work, family, and church activities. "PRIMETIME is another step in our ministry and mission," says Potts. "In addition to serving the needs of the working professional in our community, it also impacts them with a Christian message in the workplace."

PRIMETIME students must be 22 years old or older, have at least one year of work experience after high school, and have full-time employment. Degrees offered include an associate degree in business management, a bachelor of science degree in business administration, and a bachelor of science degree in management of information systems. Courses are taught one at a time, with a duration of between five and seven weeks each. The program emphasizes collaborative learning and the hands-on application of course work within the workplace.

Franc Tamboli, director of enrollment for PRIMETIME, stresses the advantages of focusing on one course at a time and the program's hands-on approach. "Learning theory shows that we are able to learn better if we fully immerse ourselves into one subject, rather than trying to master 100 different things at once," Tamboli says.

Students meet in class one evening per week for four hours and in small study groups for an additional four hours each week. Similar to a workplace environment, the program teaches teamwork in which the group draws upon each student's talents. PRIMETIME's faculty members include traditional faculty and practicing professionals, who combine academic credentials with professional expertise and familiarity with adult learning strategies.

As the PRIMETIME program helps working adults clear the academic scheduling hurdle, the program also helps with the financial aspect of a college education. Aquinas' counselors assist students in identifying various aid packages, as well as encouraging them to use their company reimbursement programs.

Aquinas' PRIMETIME program is located off campus in a state-of-the-art business park near the Nashville airport, for greater accessibility to working students. The program quickly garnered success with more than 200 working professionals attending in its inaugural year.

"Being a small college allows us to be innovative, and to move quickly and in a timely manner," says Potts. "We believe the PRIMETIME program will grow as we continue to reach out to the business community, and we are looking forward to growing in our academic degree offerings—such as baccalaureate degrees in theology and philosophy."

PRIMETIME is an accelerated, non-traditional program designed to enable working adults to finish their degree in a timely manner without sacrificing work, family, and church activities.

HCA/TriStar
Health System

*I*n 1968, Dr. Thomas F. Frist Sr. envisioned the possibility of providing compassionate, quality health care in a more affordable and convenient manner. He aimed to bring that vision to fruition, and, in doing so, changed the face of health care locally and nationally. Frist and his son, Dr. Thomas F. Frist Jr., formed a partnership with businessman Jack Massey. Together, they founded

Hospital Corporation of America (HCA), beginning with one facility–Parkview Hospital. The goal was to form a health care company that offered physicians a quality environment in which to practice. Their first office was a house on 25th Street, but it didn't take long for Frist Senior's vision to catch on–the company began expanding, buying hospitals, and merging with other companies until HCA was known in communities throughout the United States, England, and Switzerland.

Today, HCA owns and operates some 200 hospitals and other health care facilities in 23 states, England, and Switzerland. The company is bound by a mission statement: "Above all else, we are committed to the care and improvement of human life. In recognition of this commitment, we strive to deliver high-quality, cost-effective health care in the communities we serve."

To that end, HCA is dedicated to meeting each community's local health care needs. HCA is able to leverage its size and control costs by purchasing medical products in large volumes, sharing administrative costs throughout a local network, and working with physicians and caregivers to improve

The HCA corporate offices are located at One Park Plaza.

quality–often reducing redundant tests, drugs, and treatments.

Many HCA facilities have received the Joint Commission on Accreditation of Healthcare Organizations' highest rating for quality. The company credits its employees with the rating because of the quality care they deliver. HCA's values statement is taken to heart by its vast employee network: "We recognize and affirm the unique and intrinsic worth of each individual. We treat all those we serve with compassion and kindness. We act with absolute honesty, integrity, and fairness in the way we conduct our busi-

ness and the way we live our lives. We trust our colleagues as valuable members of our team and pledge to treat one another with loyalty, respect, and dignity."

HCA FOUNDATION AND COMMUNITY OUTREACH

*I*n addition, HCA employees provide hands-on involvement within the community, having volunteered more than 6,000 hours of time in various programs in 2000. Habitat for Humanity, the Juvenile Diabetes Walk-A-Thon, the Salvation Army Angel Tree, and

Team HCA walks to cure juvenile diabetes.

adopted classrooms at Brookmeade Elementary are just a sampling of the groups that benefit from the company's volunteer spirit. Through employees' generosity, HCA has raised more for United Way of Metropolitan Nashville than any other company in Middle Tennessee.

"HCA is dedicated to building stronger, healthier communities through outreach and philanthropy by working in partnership with effective non-profit organizations," says Jack Bovender, chairman and CEO of HCA. Since 1998, The HCA Foundation has targeted giving to programs for health and wellness, childhood development, and quality of life in Middle Tennessee and southern Kentucky. In 2000, the organization provided grants of some $3.26 million to more than 75 agencies and organizations.

THE TRISTAR FAMILY OF HOSPITALS

HCA's network of medical facilities in the Middle Tennessee and southern Kentucky area is the TriStar Health System. In concert with HCA's mission, TriStar is a family of 11 hospitals and medical centers that represents the forefront of medical care–providing affordable health care by consolidating business and financial services, and by allowing medical centers and hospitals to focus on what they do best, delivering quality care. The name TriStar connotes the system's three vital components–patients, physicians, and partners–which work together to create a continuum of care in the communities served.

"Our family of hospitals and medical centers in the TriStar Health System represent the forefront of medical care today," says Paul Rutledge, president of TriStar. "Our ability to share strengths, knowledge, and resources among all of our facilities gives every patient access and expertise unparalleled in the region."

TriStar maintains that its greatest strength is its geographic distribution of hospitals. The company strives to be where the people are and become a viable part of the community.

TriStar Health System is anchored by its flagship Centennial Medical Center, located in the heart of Nashville. One of Tennessee's most complete medical facilities, Centennial has 685 licensed beds and more than 1,200 physicians covering a variety of specialties. The hospital has recently received a Top 100 specialty designation by Solucient Leadership Institute, formerly known as HCIA-Sachs Institute, for superior care in the areas of stroke, orthopaedics, and breast cancer management. Centennial is one of only a small number of hospitals in the United States to earn multiple Top 100 specialty awards.

In addition to its extensive facilities, Centennial comprises three free-standing centers–The Sarah Cannon Cancer Center, The Women's Hospital at Centennial, and Parthenon Pavilion.

The Sarah Cannon Cancer Center, a landmark program, has grown to become the largest community-based, privately funded clinical research program in the country. The center that began at Centennial has expanded to a consortium of medical facilities that together offer comprehensive care from diagnosis through post-treatment care. The network of facilities located throughout Middle Tennessee and southern Kentucky enables virtually everyone in the region to access service within 30 minutes of their home.

Since 1992, the clinical trials developed at The Sarah Cannon Cancer Center have provided more than 5,000

Centennial Medical Center was recently recognized as a Top 100 hospital in the areas of stroke, orthopaedics, and breast cancer management (left).

Dr. F. Anthony Greco (center) and Dr. John D. Hainsworth (right) started the research program at The Sarah Cannon Cancer Center in 1993, with Dr. Howard A. Burris III (left) coming on board in 1997 to head up the Investigational Drug (Phase I) program (right).

Hills of Harmony

patients the opportunity to participate in cutting-edge research. The Sarah Cannon Cancer Center at Centennial Medical Center is the only facility in the Southeast to offer intense modulated radiation therapy (IMRT), which is the newest and most technologically advanced therapy available to treat cancer. IMRT uses doses of various types of radiation–stereotactic radiosurgery, stereotactic body-frame radiotherapy, 3-D conformal radiotherapy, and hyperthermia–all under one roof. The combination of these high-tech services allows physicians almost unlimited flexibility in prescribing the optimum course of therapy for each patient.

The center's namesake is Sarah Colley Cannon, who created the beloved Minnie Pearl character and whose zest for life touched the community in many ways. Cannon was diagnosed with breast cancer in 1985 and died following a stroke in 1996. In order to expand beyond the region, the Minnie Pearl Cancer Research network was formed, comprising 300 participating oncologists in 22 states.

The Women's Hospital at Centennial is the state's first hospital dedicated solely to women's health care needs, and is the second-largest obstetrics

Skyline Medical Center, TriStar Health System's newest hospital, serves the residents of northern Davidson County and southern Kentucky.

service in Middle Tennessee. The hospital provides a full spectrum of diagnostic services, 12 operating rooms, and a women's medical/surgical inpatient unit. Parthenon Pavilion at Centennial, founded in 1971, is the oldest and largest full-service, freestanding psychiatric facility in the area. The 164-bed hospital offers a comprehensive program of behavioral health services for adolescents, adults, and the elderly.

The newest member of TriStar's family is Skyline Medical Center. A striking, 386,000-square-foot medical facility constructed on one of the highest points in Davidson County, Skyline provides a panoramic view of

Hendersonville Medical Center has been honored as a top 100 hospital three times since 1995.

Nashville

downtown Nashville. Serving residents living north and east of the Cumberland River, Skyline, which opened in September 2000, features 203 private patient rooms, and is primarily known for its oncology, neurology, orthopaedics, neurosurgery, and emergency services. Additionally situated on the 59-acre campus is the Skyline Medical Plaza, a 200,000-square-foot office building containing physician offices, a pharmacy, and other health-care-related services.

Also located to the north of Nashville is TriStar's Hendersonville Medical Center, a 120-bed, community-based medical center with comprehensive medical and surgical programs. Hendersonville Medical Center was recently named one of the nation's 100 top hospitals by Solucient Leadership Institute. Serving one of Nashville's fastest-growing suburbs since 1979, Hendersonville Medical Center completed a $9 million addition in 2000 that included a new, state-of-the-art emergency department with 15 private treatment areas and a 10-bed intensive care unit.

Located due east of Nashville is Summit Medical Center, a 204-bed community hospital known for emergency care, comprehensive diabetes management, and trusted women's and obstetric services. Summit provides an extensive list of specialty care, and was recently recognized as a Top 100 Hospital in the care of breast cancer management by Solucient Leadership Institute. The entire complex is designed to focus on convenient outpatient services, as well as on intensive care services for critically ill patients.

Southern Hills Medical Center, a 160-bed hospital, has served the communities of southern Davidson, northern Rutherford, and Williamson counties since 1979. The center's strong foundation lies in its outstanding emergency, obstetrics, neurosurgery, cardiology, and orthopaedics services. In the mid-1980s, Southern Hills expanded its services to northern Rutherford County to offer physicians, diagnostics, and 24-hour-a-day/seven-day-a-week emergency care. With Rutherford County being one of the fastest-growing counties in the state, plans are under way to build a new, 75-bed facility in the Smyrna-La Vergne area, again furthering Southern Hills' commitment for offering great care closer to the community it serves.

SUPPORTING THE ENTIRE COMMUNITY

Extending its reach beyond Nashville, TriStar offers six medical facilities in outlying communities. Centennial Medical Center at Ashland City provides residents of Cheatham County access to the most comprehensive, high-quality diagnostic and emergency care. The center boasts a top 100 specialty designation for superior care in the areas of stroke, orthopaedics, and breast cancer management.

Serving Robertson and surrounding counties is the NorthCrest Medical Center, which began operations in 1956 as Jesse Holman Jones Hospital. Located in Springfield, Tennessee, NorthCrest moved to a new, 43-acre complex in 1995. The 109-bed facility represents multiple specialties supported by state-of-the-art equipment, including an in-house cardiovascular lab, a full range of outpatient services, and 24-hour emergency services. The campus includes three medical office buildings, housing approximately 50 physicians in a broad range of specialties.

For more than 40 years, Horizon Medical Center has been serving Dickson, Humphreys, and Hickman counties. Located 45 miles west of Nashville, the 176-bed community hospital offers medical/surgical care, obstetrics, gynecology, critical care, and skilled nursing services, as well as 24-hour emergency, MRI, cardiac catheterization, and outpatient services.

Located in Bowling Green, Kentucky, Greenview Regional Hospital is a 211-bed, acute care, medical-surgical facility that supplies a full-range of diagnostic, obstetrical, therapeutic, emergency, and surgical services. Serving the community since 1972, Greenview has remained a vital part of this thriving community.

River Park Hospital is the sole health care facility in McMinnville, located 70 miles southeast of Nashville. The 150,000-square-foot, 127-bed facility opened in 1996, and is designed to meet the health care needs of the residents of Warren and surrounding counties. River Park/Centennial Heart Center was opened in 2000 to meet the growing needs of these communities.

All hospitals in the TriStar Health System actively support the wellness of the communities they serve. Through free stroke assessments, blood pressure screenings, CPR classes, disease-specific programs, and senior health expo events, the hospitals complete their continuum of care and offer a valuable community service.

As Nashville and surrounding counties continue to grow, TriStar Health System will work to meet the population's diverse needs, providing affordable health care through its comprehensive delivery system. As part of HCA, TriStar's vision is to deliver high-quality, cost-effective care for the communities it serves by fostering a healing environment that includes physical, emotional, and spiritual care.

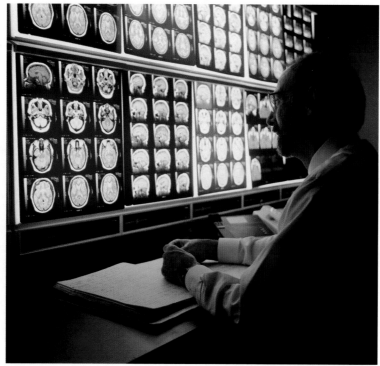

Charles L. Robinette, Jr., MD reviews X rays at Centennial Medical Center.

Comdata
Corporation

A pioneer in electronic funds disbursement and reporting technology for the transportation and retail industries, Comdata Corporation, which was founded in Nashville in 1969, has evolved into one of the largest issuers of proprietary cards used for controlled spending purchases and information services. ◆ Because Comdata is an issuer, acquirer, and processor of proprietary cards for both the

transportation and the retail sectors, the company is unlike any other. "We can provide the functionality with one card that most would take four or five to do," says Gary Krow, president of Comdata since 1999. "With one card and one system, an employee can, for example, access a secure area, receive a paycheck, get reimbursed for expenses, receive bonuses or commissions, and purchase fuel and services while on the road. No one else has all this functionality in a real-time controlled spending environment."

Companies such as the Gap/Old Navy, Kmart, JCPenney, Kroger, Exxon, Target, and many others employ Comdata's services and are a testa-ment to Comdata's success. The future remains wide open for Comdata–which generated some $310 million in sales in 2000–as the company offers an expanding portfolio of services to provide greater funds flexibility to a broader range of businesses and industries.

Comdata introduced the innovative Blue Card in 1981, which gave trucking fleets a new way to provide funds to their drivers. The Blue Card was renamed the Comchek® card in 1987. Prior to this, companies were forced to issue a company credit card, wire money, or provide cash to their drivers for fueling trucks and paying for maintenance and repairs.

With the Comchek card, drivers can pay for fuel, receive cash advances, access personal and company funds at ATMs, pay for goods at retail stores, and access long-distance telecommunications services anywhere the road takes them. In turn, the fleet company receives every piece of purchase data

With the Comchek® card from Comdata Corporation, drivers can pay for fuel, receive cash advances, access personal and company funds at ATMs, pay for goods at retail stores, and access long-distance telecommunications services anywhere the road takes them.

Comdata has been headquartered in Nashville since 1969.

generated by the driver while on the road. The fleet also uses the card as a convenient, secure driver benefit in order to attract a good workforce.

With Comdata's recent launch of Maestro® point-of-sale access to its Comchek card customers, professional drivers can now use the card at a growing number of retailers such as Wal-Mart, Walgreens, Albertson's, and the U.S. Postal Service.

Today, with more than 1 million cards in circulation, the Comchek card is the most universally accepted over-the-road fueling card in the nation. Comchek is accepted at more than 8,000 service centers and 500,000 Cirrus® ATM machines in North America.

Recently, Comdata launched Comchek® eCash, a general consumer version of the Comchek card. Comchek eCash allows companies of all sizes to streamline their payroll delivery and payment services via an electronic cash card. Companies such as Sears use Comchek eCash to disburse employee pay, while others such as Eddie Bauer use the card for termination pay.

STORED VALUE SYSTEMS

In May 2000, Comdata acquired Stored Value Systems Inc. (SVS), a leading smart card and electronic retail cash card provider. Founded as a replacement for paper gift certificates, SVS pioneered the private label gift card market by being the first company to provide broad electronic, card-based refunds and gift certificates to national department stores, gas stations, and discount retailers.

The cash card provides a great benefit to retailers because they can use the card as a promotional tool, issue the card for refunds or exchanges, and use the card for employee incentives. Ultimately, the card allows the retailer to keep more money in the store.

More than 380,000 retail locations now accept Comdata's gift cards, including a range of mass-market and midmarket retailers such as Target, JCPenney, the Gap, Kroger, Pier 1, the Limited, and Structure. All data pertaining to the gift cards is processed at Comdata's SVS office in Louisville.

TREMENDOUS INFRASTRUCTURE

Comdata has 13 locations in the United States and Canada, and employs approximately 1,800 people. With nearly 1,000 employees operating from its 450,000-square-foot office in Brentwood, Tennessee, Comdata is the largest employer in Williamson County.

Comdata's Toronto office houses the company's Permicon division, a well-known Canadian permit service. Most of the firm's other offices are regulatory compliance and authorization centers, including a bilingual center in El Paso. With call centers spread across the country and an advanced network, Comdata has the ability–with the flick of a switch–to route calls from one office to another, if necessary.

Businesses rely on Comdata's information technology (IT) know-how. "We are an extension of a company's financial department, and to an extent, their information technology department," says Krow.

Comdata employs a unique customer service program in which all managers are encouraged to "adopt a customer." On a quarterly basis, managers touch base with their customers to inquire about any problems, as well as introduce other company programs. Through a computer software program, management is kept

apprised of any concerns and comments, as well as follow-up status. This is just one of the programs that has contributed to Comdata's 92 percent customer-satisfaction rating–an unusually high rating in the financial sector.

Comdata achieves high marks for its community involvement as well. The company donates significant funds annually to charities and organizations, including the American Cancer Society, American Heart Association, March of Dimes, First Steps, United Way, and Nashville Symphony.

SUBSIDIARY OF CERIDIAN CORPORATION

In 1995, Comdata was acquired by Minneapolis-based Ceridian Corporation (NYSE:CEN), a $2 billion information services company that serves the human resources, transportation, and retail services markets. The second-largest payroll processor in the United States, Ceridian comprises Ceridian Employer Services–a provider of human resource management statements and payroll and tax filing services–and Comdata.

Over the span of three decades, Comdata has wisely managed its growth by utilizing the synergies developed in its transportation sector and by expanding into retail businesses. A Six Sigma company, Comdata remains focused on two objectives: the quality of its products and the success of its customers.

"Bottom line, we allow companies to automate and control purchases and funds distribution in a real-time environment, and we do it well," says Krow. By redefining the way money and information are moved through technology, Comdata Corporation provides an end-to-end solution for businesses, their customers, and their employees.

With nearly 1,000 employees operating from its 450,000-square-foot office in Brentwood, Tennessee, Comdata is the largest employer in Williamson County.

Businesses rely on Comdata's information technology know-how.

Volunteer State Community College

*J*ust 30 minutes north of Nashville lies a gem in the state's community college system. Situated on 100 scenic acres is Volunteer State Community College in Gallatin. Opened in 1971 as one of the first schools designed in the 31-year history of the state's community colleges, Volunteer State offers an attractive and affordable alternative to traditional four-year colleges. Volunteer State was founded when a group of concerned citizens banded together to try to get

a community college in the Gallatin area. Dr. Hal Ramer, the school's founding president, continues to serve as president today. That first year, 571 students were enrolled.

Today, the enrollment has swelled to some 7,000, and the campus features 10 attractive buildings, with plans for renovations and more on the way. With the average age of its students being 27, Volunteer State serves a number of audiences: first-generation college students, those making a career change, and those who have had life changes that have created a need for them to return to school.

Opened in 1971 as one of the first schools designed in the 31-year history of the state's community colleges, Volunteer State offers an attractive and affordable alternative to traditional four-year colleges.

A WIDE VARIETY OF OPPORTUNITIES

*V*olunteer State offers students the first two years of a four-year degree in transfer programs and a two-year associate of applied science degree, as well as a number of one- and two-year certificate programs. With classes in everything from liberal arts course work to specific programs in physical therapy, respiratory therapy, fire science, and business management, students have

many options—and all for about half the cost of a four-year public college or university.

Volunteer State boasts an experienced faculty in which all full-time instructors have at least a master's degree in their field of study; 40 to 45 percent have doctorates. Adjunct professors must have similar academic proficiency or work in their area of instruction on a full-time basis. A tribute to the school's success is that almost 30 percent of the faculty have been with the school since its inception.

Another measure of Volunteer State's success is its students who perform well in programs that require state certification; 88 percent pass within the first time of taking accreditation tests. The school itself is fully accredited by the Southern Association of Colleges and Schools, as are all programs eligible for accreditation by an outside agency.

Through an active foundation, more than 250 full- and part-time private scholarships are offered each year. Financial aid, as well as other support services such as academic advising, career counseling, mentoring, tutoring, and a wellness center, is available to students.

WIRED FOR THE 21ST CENTURY

*V*olunteer State is wired for the 21st century, as all students have free access to a computer and the Internet through the four computer labs on campus and the new, state-of-the-art library, which is connected to other libraries across the country and other colleges within the state. In 2000, Volunteer State was named by Yahoo! as one of the top wired community colleges in the nation. In addition, a number of classes are offered by videotape and on the Internet, allowing students flexibility in when they actually "go to school." To supplement the main campus, Volunteer State maintains an additional 23 off-campus sites where students can attend classes, an important aspect of a school that serves 12 counties in Middle Tennessee.

As more and more students discover the financial and academic benefits of attending Volunteer State Community College, and with 98 percent of all alumni rating the institution as excellent or good, the school is poised for excellence in the 21st century.

leading, global professional services firm, Andersen opened the doors to its Nashville office in 1976, and has built a reputation for its professionalism, technical expertise, breadth of knowledge, and commitment to client service. With some 175 employees, the office provides a wide range of services to many prominent

companies representing a variety of industries in middle and east Tennessee and western Kentucky.

With a corporate vision to be the partner for success in the new economy, Andersen strives to offer strategic business solutions through services designed with its clients' needs in mind. Andersen offers a broad range of professional services in consulting, assurance, tax, corporate finance, and, in certain countries, legal services. Andersen has consistently ranked number one in overall client satisfaction in Emerson Research Company's *Big Five U.S. Multinational Companies Client Satisfaction Study.*

The company has further distinguished itself with unique programs such as Exceeding Client Expectations Every Day (ExCEED); a Web-based knowledge service called KnowledgeSpace; Global Best Practices, which highlights optimum ways to perform business processes; and Business Risk Model.

PROFESSIONAL DEVELOPMENT

s companies embrace Andersen for its business solutions, in turn, professionals head to Andersen for an outstanding career opportunity. The Nashville office strongly supports professional development, and this commitment to training enables employees to address the changing needs of their clients with a cutting-edge approach. Each employee benefits from the excellent training offered at Andersen's premier corporate educational facility, the Center for Professional Education in St. Charles, Illinois.

Corporately, Andersen spends more than $300 million per year on professional development, which translates to more than $5,000 per employee.

The company's pledge to helping its employees succeed in their careers and maintain a healthy work/life balance is a hallmark of Andersen. Flexible work arrangements, an employee referral program, Get Well Centers offering sick care and backup care for employees' children, and a business-casual workplace environment all contribute to its *Fortune* 2000 rating as one of the 100 best companies to work for in America.

Unique initiatives, such as Continuous Assessment of Results and Expectations (CARE), support employees' professional development goals and the firm's objective of developing and retaining the best people. Growth and Retention of Women (GROW) focuses on accelerating and enhancing the recruitment, retention, advancement, and leadership paths of women through mentoring, networking, and other activities. In 2001, *Working Mother* magazine rated Andersen as one of the 100 best companies for working mothers for the ninth time.

GIVING BACK TO THE COMMUNITY

ndersen's Nashville office further instills an esprit de corps with family gatherings, holiday parties, golf tournaments, and success celebrations. The office is equally committed to the community, participating in a variety of charitable and civic activities such as Dress for Success' Clean Your Closet Week, Habitat for Humanity, Cystic Fibrosis Sports Challenge, and United Way of Metropolitan Nashville's annual fund-raising campaign. The company's Nashville office also supports the Nashville Symphony, Junior Achievement, PENCIL Foundation, Nashville's Table, and Nashville Sports Council.

Andersen's Nashville office is part of a corporate network of more than 85,000 people in 80-plus countries who are united by a single worldwide operating structure that fosters inventiveness, knowledge sharing, and a focus on client success. Since its beginning in 1913, Andersen has realized some 90 years of uninterrupted growth, with 2001 revenues reaching $9.3 billion. That kind of growth, along with the tireless dedication of its employees, is a barometer of good things to come for Andersen.

Andersen employees celebrate with the company's PENCIL partner school, Dalewood Middle, at an Andersen-sponsored picnic marking the end of the school year (top).

More than 60 Andersen employees volunteered their time to help build houses for Habitat for Humanity (bottom).

Vanderbilt Properties

*I*n a number of cities across the country, urban sprawl makes the process of finding suitable housing options that also are suitably priced increasingly difficult. Fortunately, Vanderbilt University and Brookside Properties have addressed this issue in the Nashville area with a wide range of choices for area residents. ◆ Vanderbilt Properties, the real estate arm owned by Vanderbilt University,

owns four apartment complexes and 12 homes in Hillsboro Village and midtown Nashville, highly sought after residential areas with the lowest vacancy rate in the city. Within walking distance of Vanderbilt University, a comprehensive research university, and Vanderbilt University Medical Center, these units–while not exclusive to Vanderbilt staff–attract nurses, students, physicians, and professors seeking proximity to their work. A benefit for all residents is the convenience to interstates, shopping, and restaurants, as well as attractions such as Centennial Park. Rents are attractive, with a range of housing offered to meet a variety of budgets.

OUTGROWTH OF UNIVERSITY HOUSING

*F*or years, Vanderbilt University offered housing services to students and staff, from dormitory living to apartments to single-family homes. As the largest private employer in Middle Tennessee, the university has always tried to provide assistance to its 3,700 clinical, full-, and part-time faculty, and to its staff of 12,600. Additionally, the university's community includes approximately 6,000 undergraduate and 4,100 graduate and professional students. While dormitories are now managed by Vanderbilt Student Affairs, Vanderbilt Properties was formed in 1988 to distinguish the apartments and homes owned by the university.

That same year, the flagship Village at Vanderbilt opened. The multiuse development, located on prime real estate near Hillsboro Village and across from the medical center, features 20,000 square feet of retail space, 75,000 square feet of office space, 37 town homes, and 150 apartments. At the time Village at Vanderbilt opened, it was the first new residential complex to open in the area in three years. Its luxury units were met with great enthusiasm from the city.

HOUSING OPTIONS TO MEET EVERY NEED

*W*hen development planners surveyed the area, they discovered that the number of one-bedroom apartments was limited and, therefore, two-thirds of the Village at Vanderbilt is comprised of one-bedroom units. The remaining units are two- and three-bedroom apartments. Most units offer a fireplace, and all feature traditional appointments such as a ceramic tile entry, washer/dryer connections, a dishwasher, a disposal, and other electric appliances. Residents welcome the security-controlled underground parking and around-the-clock emergency maintenance services. Central to all units is a clubhouse with a swimming pool and an exercise room. A recipient of the Beautification Award from the Greater Nashville Apartment Association, the grounds at the Village at Vanderbilt are attractively landscaped, and build-

The Village at Vanderbilt features 20,000 square feet of retail space, 75,000 square feet of office space, 37 town homes, and 150 apartments.

ings themselves complement their environs, blending nicely with the brick facades in Hillsboro Village and with the adjacent university.

Just down the street is another complex owned by Vanderbilt University–Wesley Place, which opened in 1996. Atop the Wesley Place retail/parking complex, these striking penthouse suites offer magnificent, panoramic views of the city. Vaulted ceilings, private balconies, and covered parking with card-control access add allure to these studios and one-, two-, and three-bedroom penthouses. Other amenities include ceiling fans, individual sprinkler systems, built-in microwaves, self-cleaning ovens, and washer/dryer connections.

Directly behind the Village at Vanderbilt are the Hilltop Apartments. Residents of this all-studio complex, which was originally built in 1922, enjoy the benefits of manageable rent, as well as proximity to Vanderbilt. The Barbizon Apartments, which opened in 1968, was purchased by Vanderbilt University in August 2000. The Barbizon's 45 studio and one-bedroom units have modest rents and an excellent location on Broadway, the main artery from midtown to downtown Nashville.

Vanderbilt University also owns 12 historic homes, sprinkled throughout the midtown area. All of Vanderbilt Properties' holdings are leased and managed by Brookside Properties, one of the largest real estate companies in Tennessee and one that takes great pride in providing excellent

customer service.

In addition to long-term leases, Vanderbilt Properties offers corporate suites that service two distinct markets. The fully furnished suites are available for the transient corporate market, as well as for patients at the medical center who are awaiting organ transplants, bone marrow transplants, and other critical operations. Vanderbilt Properties' corporate suites are designed to ease the stress of temporary living away from home. Residents do not have to hassle with utility connections; they are furnished, as are tele-

vision and basic cable. Bed and bath linens, all kitchen utensils, dishes and cookware, full-size washer and dryer, and weekly maid service are all included. For patients of Vanderbilt Medical Center, shuttle service to the hospital is available at no extra cost.

Through its network of properties, Vanderbilt Properties aims to provide an important service to the community–housing in the right place at the right price. Doubtless, as its collection of properties and their scope expand, Vanderbilt Properties will continue its success in this real estate niche.

The Village at Vanderbilt features a sparkling pool for its residents.

A recipient of the Beautification Award from the Greater Nashville Apartment Association, the grounds at the Village at Vanderbilt are attractively landscaped, and buildings themselves complement their environs, blending nicely with the brick facades in Hillsboro Village and with the adjacent university.

CRT, Custom Products, Inc.

riginally established in 1979 to provide quality manufacturing for the music industry, CRT, Custom Products, Inc. has diversified its products and services as it moves full force into the new century. The company now bills itself as a one-stop shop, offering manufacturing, printing, packaging, warehousing, and shipping for the music and computer software industry.

CRT, Custom Products, Inc.'s impressive 50,000-square-foot manufacturing facility is located in Whites Creek, Tennessee.

Cheryl Hutchinson, owner and president, maintains that the business was born of necessity. Her employer, California-based General Recorded Tapes, filed bankruptcy in 1979, but Hutchinson's customers wanted her to continue with the handling of their accounts. She obliged, and in the mid-1980s changed the name of the company from CRT Custom Records and Tapes to CRT, Custom Products, Inc. in order to reflect the company's growing diversity of services, rather than just the replacement of media with newer technology.

STATE-OF-THE-ART EQUIPMENT

RT takes on projects of all sizes, and will do the work from start to finish and anywhere in between. The company produces, manufactures, and packages products that include promotional posters, notebook binders, computer software boxes, compact discs, DVDs, VHS duplication, and digital business cards.

Offering full design services, the company's Desktop Department features the latest Macintosh computers that can receive files in a variety of formats.

CRT houses state-of-the-art equipment–which makes the firm's products and exemplary service stand apart–in its impressive, 50,000-square-foot manufacturing facility in Whites Creek, Tennessee. Another 22,800-square-foot building warehouses materials and finished products.

CRT's main equipment list–including prepress, printing, bindery, and packaging–is convincing and comprehensive. Offering full design services, the company's Desktop Department features the latest Macintosh computers that can receive files in a variety of formats. The firm constantly updates its capabilities with the latest and fastest formats such as QuarkXPress, PageMaker, Illustrator, and Freehand. CRT's Prepress Department boasts a Cortron that is a computerized, high-speed, step-and-repeat system accurate within 1/1,000th of an inch. Soon, the company will have the capability to go directly to plates without the need for film.

CRT's Printing Department offers six-color printing–making up to 15,000 impressions per hour–and aqueous or UV coating. The firm's Bindery Department features state-of-the-art die-cutting and embossing equipment, and its folders have capabilities up to a 32-page signature. And, finally, CRT's Packaging Department can handle single, double, or quadruple CD jewel box packaging. The CD sleever can manage up to 8,000 per hour, and its shrink-wrapper can handle 120 CD jackets per minute with on-line stickering capabilities.

CRT's Packaging Department is also able to produce customized packaging for approval before going into actual production. While the firm has fully automated operations, it still uses an assembly line for hand assembling when needed on special projects.

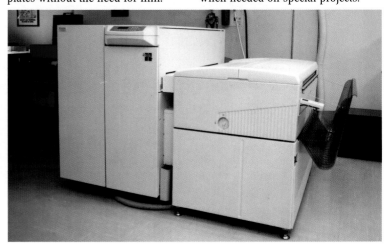

GROWTH AND SUCCESS

Quality products delivered on time are responsible for CRT's growth and success. The company's customer base is about 4,000 strong now, and includes the likes of music industry giant Sony, which employs CRT on an ongoing basis to produce its large-form posters, video boxes, and promotional compact discs. CRT works with clients throughout the United States and other parts of the world.

Hutchinson maintains that CRT has sidestepped recent economic downturns with its diverse product array. There is always something to fall back on–and currently enough work to warrant running two eight-hour shifts.

One aspect of CRT's business, though, was created because Hutchinson loves children and believes that there is not enough quality material for kids. In 1995, she launched Toy Box Productions, a label for children's audio books. Bible Stories for Kids is a series of stories told by animals and involves sing-along songs.

The Backyard Adventure Series teaches children about history in a fun, interactive way. The series features Farley's Raiders, who travel through time, encounter historic characters, and participate in exciting events. The Americana Audio Books series is targeted to older listeners, and recounts historic occurrences such as the Alamo and the Hatfield and McCoy feud.

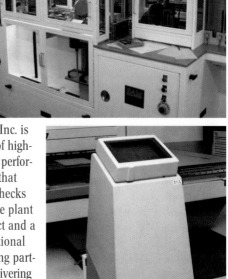

MASTERING ITS MISSION

Hutchinson's strong work ethic permeates the company and its some 100 employees. Each individual is charged with working to provide total customer satisfaction in quality, cost-effective products, and service. Employees offer friendly, reliable service to guide and assist their customers. CRT's management system–which links all departments, beginning with customer service and ending with shipping–allows for accurate communication between all departments. The e-commerce section of the system enables customers to check in real time the status of their order. Customers can even place orders directly through the system without telephone contact.

CRT's mission statement reads that "CRT, Custom Products, Inc. is dedicated to the manufacture of high-quality products with superior performance." The company backs that policy up by placing quality checks and procedures throughout the plant to ensure a top-quality product and a fully satisfied customer. Additional CRT tenets include establishing partnerships with the customer; delivering products on time; recognizing employees as the company's most valuable assets; maintaining a clean and safe working environment; being flexible in a changing business environment; and operating with truth, honesty, and integrity.

Adhering to this mission makes all employees accountable and feeling a part of a team. Together, this team serves as the driving force behind CRT's superior products and service.

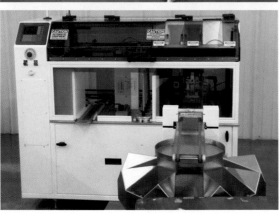

CRT places quality checks and procedures throughout the plant to ensure a top-quality product and a fully satisfied customer.

Doubletree Hotel
Nashville

H allmarks of the Doubletree Hotel include having warm cookies awaiting guests at check-in, being greeted by name by staff members ready to assist with any care or concern, and having a comfortable guest room that offers the first-class amenities many business travelers expect. A member of the Hilton family located on the Internet at

The Doubletree Hotel Nashville offers 338 guest rooms and six suites. Rooms are equipped with first-class amenities such as a dataport, two telephone lines, voice mail, a coffee-maker, and Neutrogena bath products. Several of the rooms are compliant with the Americans with Disabilities Act, featuring roll-in showers and lift chairs.

www.doubletree.com, the Doubletree Hotel Nashville has been situated in the heart of the city's downtown business district since 1979. A Mobil three-star property, the hotel delivers on the expectations and standards of Hilton, while offering the comfortable style of Doubletree.

The cookies are a guest's first sign that this hotel is truly a home away from home. It's a welcome respite after a day of travel, and presents an excellent opportunity for dialogue between hotel staff and guests. And unlike their counterparts at many other hotels, Doubletree staff members are empowered to make decisions and solve a customer's problem without having to refer to senior management. Staff members can enact a 100 percent guarantee, and ensure that every customer leaves feeling great about his or her stay at Doubletree.

Doubletree staff members also comprise the hotel's Care Committee. "The purpose of this group is to see what they can do to enrich the lives of the customer, the community, and their peers," says Gene Anderson, general manager. The Care Committee enacts customer recognition programs and employee events that boost morale,

as well as allowing members to support a range of charities through volunteer and fund-raising efforts.

Doubletree prides itself on its diversity within the ranks, and reaches out to employ a number of adults with disabilities. "These employees are one aspect of diversity that many hotels miss," says Anderson. "Our hotel celebrates Nashville's diversity."

EXTRAORDINARY, NOT ORDINARY

W ith 15,000 square feet of meeting space–80 percent of which is on one level–Doubletree is ideally suited for smaller groups of 50 to 300 people. In an effort to make groups feel welcome during their stay, the hotel's staff members will carry out a theme relevant to the group's interest. That has included everything from displaying welcome banners at the front desk to changing the decor of the restaurant and the uniforms of the hotel staff. "We work hard to make each event unique," notes Anderson. "It's what makes us extraordinary, not ordinary."

Because of the property's convenient downtown location, Doubletree is also popular with guests who are attend-

ing performances at the Tennessee Performing Arts Center, going to Titans football games, or visiting famous Nashville landmarks. Additionally, special packages such as the Romance Package, which features a Crabtree & Evelyn gift basket, attract couples celebrating anniversaries and the like.

Contemporary in design and featuring a unique triangular exterior, the 10-story Doubletree offers 338 guest rooms and six suites. Rooms are equipped with first-class amenities such as a dataport, two telephone lines, voice mail, a coffeemaker, and Neutrogena bath products. Several of the rooms are compliant with the Americans with Disabilities Act, featuring roll-in showers and lift chairs. The hotel also houses a restaurant and bar, a full-service gift shop, and a health club with a swimming pool. All guests can take advantage of the industry-leading Hilton HHonors awards program, in which points can be accrued for mileage and overnight stays, and exchanged for a myriad of gifts.

With its uncompromising service and comfortable style, the Doubletree Hotel Nashville embraces its customers and keeps them coming back for more.

Profiles in Excellence

1981   THE CROMWELL GROUP, INC.

1983   UNION PLANTERS BANK

1984   BELLSOUTH TELECOMMUNICATIONS, INC.

1984   CENTEX HOMES

1984   LOEWS VANDERBILT HOTEL

1985   NASHVILLE BUSINESS JOURNAL

1985   SHERATON MUSIC CITY HOTEL

1986   COMMUNITY HEALTH SYSTEMS, INC.

1986   SOUTHWEST AIRLINES

1987   RENAISSANCE NASHVILLE HOTEL

1988   AIRPORT RAMADA INN & SUITES

1991   TENNESSEE DEPARTMENT OF ENVIRONMENT AND CONSERVATION

1992   CURB RECORDS INC.

1996   XO COMMUNICATIONS, INC.

2000   CITADEL COMMUNICATIONS CORPORATION

1980–2002

The Cromwell Group, Inc.

The Cromwell Group, Inc. operates Nashville's The Buzz® 102.9 FM (WBUZ-FM) and The Party® 102.5 FM (WQZQ-FM), targeting listeners ages 18 to 44, while focusing on the kind of citizens those listeners will become 10 and 20 years from now. The Buzz and The Party know that their listeners today are the community leaders of tomorrow; therefore, the stations strive to impact the lives of their

Personalities from Nashville's The Buzz® 102.9 FM (WBUZ-FM) and The Party® 102.5 FM (WQZQ-FM) emcee various activities throughout the community.

The two stations, in conjunction with local firefighters, armed forces, and other organizations, sent a truckload of needed supplies to New York in response to the September 11, 2001, disaster at the World Trade Center (left).

The Buzz and The Party support a variety of local charities, including the YW's Women's Domestic Shelter, Special Olympics, Child Abuse Prevention Center, and many others (right).

audience by sharing positive messages, linking arms with the community, playing popular music, and listening and responding to the audience. Since bursting onto the Nashville scene in 1997, The Buzz and The Party, each with 100,000 watts of power, have made a tremendous impact on the consistently growing audience of young people in Middle Tennessee. The Buzz reaches an 18-to-44 age group that is mostly male, while the Party reaches a more female audience of the same age group. Both stations generate a significant amount of teen and parent listenership.

LOCALLY OWNED AND OPERATED

In business since 1972, the Cromwell Group has launched more than 25 radio stations in small and medium-sized communities in Illinois, Kentucky, Tennessee, and Indiana, while operating from its home base in Nashville. In 1990, a Cromwell Group affiliate purchased the 3,000-watt WQZQ 102.5, originally licensed to Dickson, Tennessee. Cromwell slowly moved the station to 50,000 watts, and then to 100,000 watts, before launching

The Party in 1997. WQZQ-FM is now licensed to Pegram, Tennessee.

Similarly, WBUZ 102.9–licensed to Shelbyville, Tennessee, and later to LaVergne, Tennessee–was purchased in 1989. Its tower was moved to Williamson County to enable the station to transmit at 100,000 watts and cover the Nashville metro area. In 1997, the tower height was increased further, and The Buzz launched a new era in rock music in Nashville. Today, The Party and The Buzz are two of only 12 FM stations in Nashville that transmit at 100,000 watts. The stations can be heard for 70 miles around Nashville–throughout

Middle Tennessee and into Kentucky and northern Alabama.

The Cromwell Group's 28-plus Nashville employees feel a sense of responsibility to be active in the community. They not only are involved in quality-of-life issues in the midstate area, but also want to instill that activism and volunteer spirit within their young adult audiences.

MORE THAN MUSIC

The Cromwell Group's Nashville listeners tune to The Party and The Buzz to hear their favorite songs. In between, they get information about what's going on in Middle Tennessee. From breast cancer awareness to community government, the stations' on-air personalities spread the word about causes and concerns relevant to the Middle Tennessee public.

"We are blessed with an opportunity," says Bayard Walters, president of the Cromwell Group. "We are able to shape or join in a way that the average person cannot. We want to seize this opportunity to get a positive message across."

During election year and in an ongoing campaign, the stations have a massive voter registration drive for

young adults and invite candidates to appear on The Party's popular *Morning Show.* At The Buzz-sponsored Dancin' in the District, a weekly summer concert staged at Riverfront Park, employees of The Party and The Buzz attempt to register just about everyone to vote.

The Party operates a separate alcohol-free zone–the Smooth Zone–at Dancin' in the District in order to give people under age 21, or those who do not want to drink, an alternative place to hang out, dance, play interactive games, and have fun with the on-air personalities. The Smooth Zone was an instant success with thousands in attendance on its inaugural year and throughout the following seasons.

THE NEXT GENERATION

A signature event for the Cromwell Group's Nashville stations is Mayor's First Day, held in conjunction with the Mayor's Youth Council. The Buzz and The Party were the first radio stations to sign on to this event, which encourages parents to get involved with their kids and to go to school with them on their first day of classes.

Hosts of The Party's *Morning Show* have served as official spokespersons for the AIDS Walk sponsored by Nashville Cares. Every year, the station supports the cause with significant radio time and encourages listener participation.

The Cromwell Group's Nashville stations utilize their colorful box trucks at promotions and events throughout the city, opening up to six events per day per station. Whether assisting the Red Cross in blood drives, raising money from concerts for the YW's Domestic Violence Center, sending free doughnuts and water for cleanup crews following the Clarksville tornado, or partnering with a mall for an A-Team promotion–a party for students who receive good grades–The Buzz and the Party give it their all.

Behind the scenes, the Cromwell Group's Nashville stations support many causes on their own. In an event closed to the public, The Party sends on-air personalities and goody bags to the Foster Parents Picnic put on by the State Department of Children's Services. The stations frequently assist their neighborhood school, Una Elementary, and offer job-shadowing opportunities for high school and

college students who are interested in the radio business.

The Buzz and The Party also support two of Music City's favorite pastimes–sports and music. The stations host parties and distribute goody bags at various Nashville team (Sounds, Predators, and Titans) home games. Every Sunday night, The Buzz airs *Local Buzz,* a show featuring the music of unsigned bands and musicians, providing a creative outlet for these talented performers.

"Right now, our audience is very active on the Internet (1029TheBuzz.com or 1025TheParty.com), e-mailing us with suggestions, comments, and questions on a daily basis," adds Walters. "We respond to all those e-mails. It's important to us to get involved on a personal level." That personal rapport with the audience is what sets the Cromwell Group, Inc.'s Nashville stations–The Buzz and The Party–apart as they work to positively influence the city's next generation of leaders.

The Cromwell Group, Inc. and its affiliates are an equal opportunity employer. Locally owned in Nashville, the company operates more than 20 radio stations in Illinois, Kentucky, Tennessee, and Indiana.

The stations' trucks and vans are seen supporting events throughout the area (left).

BuzzFest features 20 bands on two stages, in addition to games and merchandise booths (right).

Listeners and contest winners are regularly taken to lunch in The Party limousine.

Union Planters Bank

W hen attempting to describe the approach of Union Planters Bank of Nashville, Ron Samuels, CEO and president, highlights the intelligence of a big bank with the sensitivity of a smaller bank. Union Planters Corp., a 12-state holding company, currently has assets of some $35 billion. While ranking among the nation's top 30 banks, Union

Planters maintains a vision and values that reflect the heart and soul of community banking: people still matter.

Union Planters' customer-focused philosophy is one that sets it apart, and is central to the bank's growth and success since establishing itself in Nashville in 1983. The company actually has a long and storied past that dates back to its 1869 founding by a group of businessmen in Memphis. Under the leadership of William Farrington, the group was ready to convert a small marine and fire insurance company into a new institution they named the Union and Planters Bank of Memphis.

The name was derived from two formerly successful banks in Memphis—Branch Union and Branch Planters—intimating that the new bank would have the combined strength of the two. At the time, Memphis was in need of banks, so the offering of stock was met

with great enthusiasm. The bank endured through the years, weathering good times and bad–financial panic, depression, world wars, and the technology age. Today, Union Planters is one of the largest bank holding companies with headquarters in Tennessee.

In 1983, Union Planters acquired the failed United Southern Bank in Nashville from the FDIC, and quickly began spreading its roots throughout the city. In 1992, the company acquired Fidelity Bancshares in Nashville, along with the $585 million in deposits of Metropolitan Federal Savings and Loan, a Nashville thrift with 17 branches. Today, Union Planters has 36 full-service branch locations in the metropolitan Nashville area and more than 50 ATMs.

EXCEEDING EXPECTATIONS

A full-service financial services organization, Union Planters strives to provide long-term, high-performance service in a competitive, rapidly changing business environment. The company's 500-plus Nashville employees are well trained and are committed to finding financial solutions for their customers–solutions that not only meet, but ex-

Union Planters Bank's Nashville operation is led by (from left) Kent Cleaver, executive vice president, commercial division; Ron Samuels, president and CEO; and Bruce Hammond, executive vice president, retail division.

Union Planters' Nashville headquarters is located on Union Street.

ceed customer expectations. By having a team of employees who listen to their customers and who respond with knowledgeable, practical solutions, Union Planters is a bank where business as usual is simply not good enough. The U.S. Small Business Administration has named Union Planters as one of the nation's most friendly small-business lenders, ranking it third among the 50 largest bank holding companies.

Maintaining sensitivity to customers, while also providing the best of technological and bank service offerings found typically in large banks, has been instrumental in Union Planters' success. Whether the bank's customers are in search of traditional banking products, including mortgages, home equity loans, or checking and savings accounts, or the customer is a growing business, Union Planters offers a broad range of products that can be tailored to meet individual needs.

Union Planters offers state-of-the-art conveniences like Internet banking, online bill pay, and telephone banking. The bank's UPBusiness Express is an electronic banking service specifically designed for small and midsize businesses that can manage their banking and financial transactions via personal computers, while exercising greater control over cash balances and increasing productivity.

Through Union Planters Financial Services, customers have access to a full range of investment opportunities to secure retirement, a child's education, or whatever investment objectives customers may have. Licensed branch specialists are available to help individuals understand and choose the investment best suited for their needs.

For those who require comprehensive personal service, Union Planters Private Banking offers many advantages such as special investor accounts, discounted pricing on trust and brokerage services, preferred lines of credit, and exclusively designated relationship managers to help maximize time and money.

Additionally, Union Planters Trust and Investment Management offers options that include a full range of personal trust, investment management, and retirement plan services. Through Union Planters Insurance Agency, individuals can select from a wide spectrum of competitively priced insurance products.

Union Planters' combination of

Union Planters gives back to the community in many ways, including participation in the American Cancer Society's Relay for Life (top) and the bowlathon benefiting Junior Achievement (left).

superior products with a delivery system that is fast, responsive, and efficient adds up to a bank that delights in delighting its customers.

COMMUNITY IMPACT

*I*n addition to serving its customers, Union Planters is dedicated to serving its community. Union Planters' employees have formed Individuals Making Progress and Changing Tomorrow (IMPACT), a nationally recognized volunteer program that encourages employees to provide volunteer service to their respective communities. Union Planters Nashville employees volunteered more than 1,600 hours in 2000.

Besides supporting a multitude of local charities, Union Planters is involved in initiatives for community outreach—including projects designed to assist citizens in acquiring affordable

housing and in carrying out home rehabilitation projects—sponsored by such organizations as the Fannie Mae Foundation, Affordable Housing Resources, and Metropolitan Development and Housing Association. Union Planters is participating in a program to build 99 new homes in every part of the state and, through March 2001, had made more than $260 million in loans through its Affordable Housing product.

"The future is bright and promising for Nashville and for Union Planters Bank," says Samuels. "We're determined to help create as many wins as possible for this city."

By building relationships—with the community, clients, associates, and business partners—and becoming a trusted financial adviser, Union Planters Bank is dedicated to creating a more vibrant and productive Nashville.

BellSouth
Telecommunications, Inc.

*P*roviding high-tech solutions and serving the community go hand in hand at BellSouth Telecommunications, Inc. While contributing volunteer time and more than $3 million annually to charitable and civic causes in Tennessee, BellSouth works to meet the needs of businesses and residences throughout the Nashville area by providing a full array of broadband data

and e-commerce solutions such as Web hosting and other Internet services, as well as high-speed Internet access and advanced voice features.

BellSouth Tennessee was founded in 1984, and is a part of BellSouth Corporation, an integrated communications services company. BellSouth, headquartered in Atlanta, serves more than 41 million customers in the United States and 16 other countries. A Fortune 100 company with total revenues exceeding $26 billion, BellSouth is consistently recognized for customer satisfaction.

STAYING CONNECTED

*B*ellSouth has developed a network infrastructure featuring widespread deployment of fiber-optic facilities and digital switching in every exchange, and has installed more than 403,000 miles of fiber-optic lines in Tennessee. The company's integrated voice/data network is designed to withstand natural disaster as much as it is humanly possible to do so, as well as to provide immediate response when disasters occur. BellSouth's fiber-optic cable is installed in a ring architecture, which improves service and assures reliability for business and residential customers. Further, BellSouth annually invests some $350 million to grow and modernize its Tennessee infrastructure to ensure the integrity of its service.

Whether for a small business or a large university, BellSouth can provide high-speed connectivity to the Internet through its digital subscriber line (DSL) service.

With BellSouth's state-of-the-art DSL technology–at speeds 50 times faster than standard dial-up service–the Internet connection is always on. This means no dial-up delays, no annoying busy signals, and no drop-offs in service. Customers have a dedicated connection–rather than cable modems–which means guaranteed bandwidth, consistent download speeds, and peace of mind when transmitting important files. DSL users are able to talk on the phone and surf the Internet at the same time.

Committed to meeting customer demand for high-speed Internet access, BellSouth has aggressive plans to expand deployment of additional

BellSouth Telecommunications, Inc. works to meet the needs of businesses and residences throughout Tennessee by providing a full array of broadband data and e-commerce solutions such as Web hosting and other Internet services, as well as high-speed Internet access and advanced voice features.

Nashville

BellSouth contributes more than $3 million annually to charitable and civic causes in Tennessee. The BellSouth Pioneers, for example, donated hundreds of Hug-a-Bears to the Metropolitan Police Department domestic violence unit and to the YWCA's Domestic Violence Center.

central offices and remote neighborhood solutions to enable DSL services to reach a broader consumer base.

"In Tennessee, BellSouth's network is the foundation of the digital or networked economy," says Marty Dickens, president of BellSouth in Tennessee. "Through our technology, our customers now have access to tools that, just a few years ago, only the biggest corporations and agencies could afford. Our network continues to be an opportunity-producing machine for the people and businesses of the state."

SPIRIT OF GIVING

There is more to reliable telecommunications than technology: it takes people, too, and BellSouth has nearly 3,000 employees in Middle Tennessee. The BellSouth Pioneers–the company's volunteer service organization, comprising both active and retired employees–logs more than 1 million hours of volunteer time on projects in Tennessee communities every year. Through charitable contributions and participation in community civic activities, BellSouth works to improve the quality of life in areas such as education, health and human services, and arts and culture.

The BellSouth Pioneers, for example, donated hundreds of Hug-a-Bears to the Metropolitan Police Department domestic violence unit and to the YWCA's Domestic Violence Center. The organization also helped assemble a new, more accessible play area for children attending High Hopes, a re-

source center and preschool for children with special needs.

Recognizing that today's kids are tomorrow's leaders, BellSouth makes it a priority to ensure that students have the tools they need to continue learning and competing. The company is investing $100 million throughout the Southeast to create a more dynamic learning environment and to get schools, teachers, and classrooms on-line and in touch. From Homework Hotline in Nashville to the Governor's Study Partner Program, BellSouth strives to build the future today.

In addition, the popular BellSouth Senior Classic, held annually in Nashville, has generated more than $1.3 million in proceeds for 15 Middle Tennessee agencies over the past seven years, improving life for countless Nashville families.

The BellSouth Foundation has awarded $2.5 million to Tennessee's educational institutions since 1991.

For 2001 to 2005, the company's focus is on two programs: Closing the Divide–for disadvantaged high school students, college-bound minorities, and technology-disadvantaged communities; and Forging New Paths–for Latin America's children, teachers, and leaders, as well as technology and learning.

BellSouth has also formalized an initiative to sponsor small, minority-owned, and women-owned businesses and organizations throughout the state. The initiative helps provide the resources these businesses need to flourish: capital, expertise, access to new technology, and dozens of forums for networking.

"For more than a century we've taken the latest in communications technology and turned it to the advantage of our customers," says F. Duane Ackerman, chairman and CEO of BellSouth Corporation. "Today, we continue that heritage in the digital era. The computer has joined the telephone at the heart of our business, and we're enabling businesses and consumers to use a wide range of new tools made possible by the Internet and wireless technology."

Connect and Create Something is a fitting slogan for a company that, in addition to its commitment to civic and charitable causes, brings value to the community through its innovative products and services. BellSouth Telecommunications, Inc. helps to make lives simpler and more meaningful for the region's families, schools, and businesses.

Marty Dickens serves as president of of BellSouth of Tennessee.

Centex Homes

entex Homes has made its presence well known since opening a division in the Nashville area in 1984. Having built subdivisions and homes in Sumner, Wilson, Davidson, and Williamson counties, Centex has remained true to its mission statement, which says that the purpose of Centex Homes is to build quality homes and neighborhoods that exceed the expectations established with the company's customers.

By staying on top of trends and delivering a quality product, Centex has garnered an outstanding reputation with Realtors and home buyers in the area. Centex services a wide variety of price points and markets, building for the first-time buyer, as well as executive homes.

Centex Homes has made its presence well known since opening a division in the Nashville area in 1984.

Centex's on-site architectural staff is continually open to new ideas, keeping up with buyers' wants and needs. Popular features such as bonus rooms, structured wiring, home offices, great rooms, additional storage space, and two-story living spaces are incorporated into the home designs. Even Centex's entry-level homes include nice features such as walk-in closets and baths with a separate shower and garden tub. All Centex homes are backed with a special 10-year warranty program. The result for Centex is an outstanding referral rate and a growing market share in the area.

MAJOR MILESTONES

Centex Homes was founded in Dallas in 1950 as a division of Centex Construction Company, a residential and commercial builder. Since its inception, Centex

Throughout its rapid growth, Centex Homes has remained committed to its customers and dedicated to providing the features they expect.

Homes has been on the leading edge of technological advances in construction. In the 1950s, Centex Homes began development of the nation's first master-planned community, Elk Grove Village, Illinois. This new "city" debuted in 1957 with such innovations as the first underground utilities and phone lines. Elk Grove Village has since grown into a prosperous Chicago suburb.

Centex Corporation was incorporated in 1968, and the company began trading stock publicly (NYSE:CTX) a year later. Centex Homes became a separate business unit dedicated to residential construction.

To date, Centex Homes has built more than 300,000 homes and expanded into more than 75 metropolitan markets, 22 states, and Washington, D.C. In 1998, Centex became the first U.S. home builder to expand into the United Kingdom, with the acquisition of Fairclough Homes.

Throughout its rapid growth, Centex Homes has remained committed to its customers and dedicated to providing the features they expect. Centex Homes is the only builder to rank among the top 10 on *Professional Builder's* Giant 400 list each year since its inception in 1968. In 1998,

the magazine named Centex its Builder of the Year.

In 2000, *Fortune* recognized Centex Corporation as the country's most admired company in the magazine's Engineering and Construction category. Also in 2000, Salomon Smith Barney added Centex Corporation to its Future Economy Portfolio, saying that Centex is among the most sophisticated and Internet-savvy companies in the market, and will best be able to integrate attributes of the old and new economy into the future economy.

THE EMPLOYEE DIFFERENCE

Centex's Nashville division boasts a customer service rating that is second in the nation out of the company's 44 corporate divisions. With more than 40 employees–including members of its sister company, CTX Mortgage–the office has built a strong team. The Nashville group has the least employee turnover for any division of Centex–an accomplishment in an industry where people are frequently making career moves.

Centex makes training a priority in all departments. From construction and engineering to sales, employees

are constantly learning the latest innovations, methods, and products. All work hard to fulfill the company's goal of satisfied customers who recommend Centex Homes without reservation.

COMMITMENT TO NASHVILLE

As one of the first national builders to come to Nashville, Centex remains committed to the area. While many other national builders have come and gone, Centex is focusing on growth in Middle Tennessee, with plans to expand into new price points, markets, and subdivisions. The company has recently become involved in the multifamily arena.

With its growth and success, Centex Homes–both on a local and a national level–believes in an obligation to society and to the communities in which its employees live and work. In Nashville, Centex has participated in building six Habitat for Humanity homes. Further, a portion of the sale of every Centex home is earmarked for the Nature Conservancy, the private sector leader in purchasing and preserving land for future generations. The company also actively contributes to the Make-A-Wish Foundation, United Way, and National Housing Endowment.

More than 50 years of Centex Homes' home-building experience and the company's commitment to meeting and exceeding home buyers' expectations are key ingredients in the promise of "Centex certainty."

Popular features such as bonus rooms, structured wiring, home offices, great rooms, additional storage space, and two-story living spaces are incorporated into the home designs.

Loews Vanderbilt Hotel

*S*tand outside the Loews Vanderbilt Hotel in Nashville and any type of guest can be seen pulling up to the valet entrance. Celebrities step out of limousines, corporate executives hop out of taxis, and entire families climb out of SUVs. Few hotels cater to as diverse a clientele as Loews, but one thing is the same for everyone who enters the hotel: a unique and memorable experience. ◆ From

blue-chip meetings to black-tie balls, Loews superbly accommodates groups from 12 to 1,200. The 23,000-square-foot meeting and function space includes two boardrooms with conference tables, broadcast-quality lighting and sound systems, a sophisticated ballroom, and an expansive, 3,900-square-foot, prefunction promenade.

Since 1984, Loews has been entertaining guests the way friends entertain friends. At Loews, the music one hears after stepping through the door–often that of the many celebrities who have stayed there–is just the beginning.

ELEGANCE THROUGHOUT

*T*ouchable elegance is evident throughout the hotel. In the stylish marble lobby, colonnades rise up 30 feet, creating a dramatic entrance in a space adorned by stunning artwork and exquisite floral arrangements. Guests are greeted by a friendly and helpful staff, and given the feeling that they are welcome to linger and relax for as long as they like.

Off the main lobby, Kraus Art Gallery showcases bold, colorful paintings, and has become a popular place for browsing and buying. Carol G's Salon and Day Spa offers complete hair, nail, and skin service, as well as pampering experiences, including classic massages and exotic treatments. Ginnette's Boutique features clothing and accessories, and the hotel gift shop is stocked with sundries and souvenirs.

The hotel's full-service restaurant, eat, features American and New South cuisine. The hotel's lobby bar and patio, drink, offers live piano entertainment, beverages, and light snacks in the evening, and a coffee/pastry service in the morning. Ruth's Chris

Touchable elegance is evident throughout the Loews Vanderbilt Hotel.

Steakhouse, known nationwide for its rich and hearty steaks, operates a location in the hotel's lower level, with an entrance onto the street.

GETTING DOWN TO BUSINESS

*L*oews caters to both business and leisure travelers by offering rooms designed with both types of guest in mind. An exclusive lounge area and full concierge

service are dedicated to the top three floors of the 11-story, 340-room hotel. Each room of the hotel is decorated with rich furnishings and fabrics, and all rooms are equipped with CD players, coffeemakers, minibars, hair dryers, irons and ironing boards, umbrellas, safes, and even cowboy hats for guests who really want to get into the Nashville experience. For the guest who desires luxurious accommodations, there are 13 magnificent suites, some with private French balconies, working fireplaces, wet bars, and stunning views of Nashville.

Rooms on designated business-class floors include high-speed Internet access, fax machines, dual-line phones, and voice mail. State-of-the-art office equipment, including the most current software packages, is available for use in the hotel's Executive Business Center. Small groups meeting at the hotel may also use Loews Access, a personalized, one-stop shopping service in which one hotel representative makes all of the arrangements for the group–from booking guest rooms to securing the right meeting space to organizing banquets.

The hotel's concierge is available to direct guests and help make arrangements for entertainment outside the hotel. And, while staying at Loews, the concierge can provide items from the Loews Closet, which is filled with things a guest might have forgotten to bring from home.

HEART OF NASHVILLE

Conveniently located in the heart of Nashville's business and medical community, Loews is also directly across from Vanderbilt University, minutes from Music Row, and less than two miles from downtown. The hotel is close to major attractions such as the Parthenon, Belle Meade Plantation, Frist Center for the Visual Arts, Country Music Hall of Fame, the State Capitol, Bicentennial Mall, Ryman Auditorium, Gaylord Entertainment Center, Adelphia Coliseum, and Cheekwood Fine Arts and Botanical Gardens. Guests can also walk to many restaurants, ranging

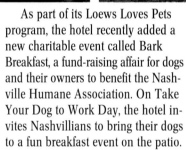
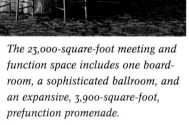

from fast food to fine cuisine, located in the area.

At the heart of Loews' success is its commitment to taking good care of its guests and its dedication to giving good care to the community. Through its Good Neighbor Policy, the hotel has gained a reputation for its charitable spirit.

Each year, at Loews Loves Kids, the hotel's ballroom fills with children from around the community who join to make gift bags for patients at Vanderbilt Children's Hospital. A Gingerbread World, the hotel's annual competition and display of gingerbread houses, benefits the Dede Wallace Center, and has raised more than $400,000 since 1984.

As part of its Loews Loves Pets program, the hotel recently added a new charitable event called Bark Breakfast, a fund-raising affair for dogs and their owners to benefit the Nashville Humane Association. On Take Your Dog to Work Day, the hotel invites Nashvillians to bring their dogs to a fun breakfast event on the patio.

Women on the Path to Success is a daylong career workshop and make-over event that helps women on public assistance transition into careers by providing job search information, tips on interviewing, makeovers, advice on dressing for success, and an opportunity to learn about careers in the hospitality industry.

Based on its constant commitment to enhancing customer service and the customer experience, Loews formed an advisory council in 1990 that meets quarterly to discuss, analyze, and make recommendations for improving the hotel and its programs. The hotel also sponsors two focus groups each year to keep informed about trends in the travel market.

Loews Vanderbilt Hotel is one of the most successful properties in the Loews chain of 17 hotels and resorts. Loews' emphasis on creating a memorable experience for its guests and its dedication to the community are evident as the hotel strives to be a good friend to its clientele and a good neighbor in Nashville.

The 23,000-square-foot meeting and function space includes one boardroom, a sophisticated ballroom, and an expansive, 3,900-square-foot, prefunction promenade.

Each room of the hotel is decorated with rich furnishings and fabrics, and all rooms are equipped with CD players, coffeemakers, minibars, hair dryers, irons and ironing boards, umbrellas, safes, and even cowboy hats for guests who really want to get into the Nashville experience.

Nashville Business Journal

A vital tool for doing business in the Nashville area, the *Nashville Business Journal*, a weekly newspaper founded in 1985, distinguishes itself with its in-depth reporting of businesses in the nine-county Middle Tennessee area. ◆ "We have a very specific focus," says Bill McMeekin, publisher. "We're all about local businesses.

Clockwise from top:
The Nashville Business Journal *is a vital tool for doing business in Middle Tennessee.*

Editor Kenneth Pybus (center) and Publisher Bill McMeekin (right) discuss area business developments on a local morning radio talk show.

The news staff of the Nashville Business Journal *provide in-depth coverage of the area's business community.*

We don't try to be all things to all people, but want to be the best source of local business news and information. We want to break the news, but also explain it. Because we have more time and space, we can provide more depth, insight, and analysis."

While the *Nashville Business Journal* is very much a local company focusing on local business, it is owned by American City Business Journals, a company that publishes papers in 41 of the top 50 markets across the country. The company acquired the *Nashville Business Journal* from Mid-South Communications in 1997.

REPORTING THE NEWS

Instead of relying on wire service stories, the *Nashville Business Journal* has a dedicated newsroom staff who generate about 95 percent of the weekly content. Each reporter is assigned a beat, and is expected to become the eyes and ears of the particular industry he or she covers. "We want our reporters to develop a certain level of sophistication in that industry, but be able to explain it to a general business audience," says McMeekin. "We present lesson-driven stories on entrepreneurs

and on small businesses and growth companies."

In addition to bringing compelling local stories to the forefront, the *Nashville Business Journal* provides a powerful vehicle for businesses to get their message out to the community through advertisements. On a weekly basis, the paper spotlights a particular industry, and offers regular features, which create an optimum advertising environment.

Research components such as *Market Facts* and the weekly *Top 20 List* provide relevant statistical and demographic data. *Achievers* highlights individual honors, and *For the Record* details judgments, bankruptcies, real estate transactions, and other public record information. Weekly focus sections provide analysis and insight into specific industries, including real estate, finance, health care, and technology.

MORE THAN A WEEKLY PAPER

The *Nashville Business Journal* also provides news in a real-time environment. The newspaper's Web site at nashville.bcentral.com provides updated and breaking stories through-

out the day, and is particularly helpful in its coverage of public companies. Subscribers to the *Nashville Business Journal* may also choose to receive a daily update by e-mail.

The company produces several annual publications, including one on the area's top 100 private companies. Its annual *Book of Lists* is a compilation of all the weekly *Top 20 Lists* and is a great resource for businesses. In 2001, the company produced more than 20 special publications geared to specific industries or related to research. Each year, the *Business Journal* hosts events for the business community that feature panel discussions, expert speakers, and networking mixers.

Financially, the *Nashville Business Journal* has experienced a great period of growth since 1997, and has seen weekly readership grow steadily to more than 31,000. Plans for the future include a more concentrated effort to expand coverage and circulation in the rest of Middle Tennessee with the same vim and vigor the company exerts in metropolitan Nashville. An increased Web presence and more focus on technology are also part of the company's goals as it continues to weave itself within the fabric of Nashville's business community.

uilt on the basic premise that hometown hospitals are vital to the community's health status, Community Health Systems, Inc. (CHS) has breathed life into struggling community hospitals by privatizing them, infusing capital, recruiting physicians, and controlling expenses. CHS has parlayed its successful strategy to approximately 55

hospitals in 20 states, making the company one of the largest non-urban providers of general hospital health care services in the United States in terms of number of facilities and revenues. In more than 85 percent of its markets, CHS is the sole provider of general hospital health care services.

The payoff CHS brings to the community is tremendous. Residents do not have to travel to neighboring towns for acute hospital care services. Physicians recruited to the hospital contribute to the talent pool, as well as providing an economic boost to the area. The hospital receives substantial technological upgrades and rids itself of the financial burdens of being a stand-alone facility. "We bring value through our size, experience, and administrative efficiencies that a small, individual facility could never hope to achieve on its own," says Wayne Smith, chairman, president, and CEO.

Founded in Houston in 1985, CHS opened an office in Nashville in 1986 and moved its headquarters to Nashville in 1996. The company has seen revenues grow from $38 million in 1986 to more than $1.3 billion in 2000. CHS was a publicly traded company for five years before becoming a private company in 1996, when its stock was purchased by Affiliates of Forstmann Little & Company. In June 2000, CHS completed an initial public offering of its common stock on the New York Stock Exchange and is traded under the symbol CYH.

A Partnership

Whether its hospitals are leased or owned, CHS considers the relationship a partnership because of the company's desire to maintain significant com-

munity involvement. CHS is a welcome addition to local communities. Further, the company retains a local board of directors, made up exclusively of the citizens and physicians of that community, for each of its hospitals. CHS does not implement cookie-cutter programs, but rather pilots different programs in various hospitals to determine what will and what will not work in a particular community.

Smith says, "What we do well is to rally a community effort behind each of our hospitals—often retaining its original name and identity, rather than branding it—and then we standardize and centralize the things that will help that hospital succeed."

For example, when CHS purchased Moberly Regional Medical Center in Moberly, Missouri, in 1993 from a not-for-profit system, the hospital was several million dollars in the red, the medical staff had expressed discontent, and physician recruitment efforts were challenging. CHS has invested more than $4 million in the hospital to upgrade equipment, and has recruited physicians in the areas of internal medicine, family practice, pediatrics, obstetrics/ gynecology, and cardiology. The end result has been a significant increase in outpatient and emergency room

services. While CHS hospitals can treat a majority of health problems, they establish relationships with major tertiary care centers to refer patients who require complicated medical intervention.

A validation of CHS' efforts is the outstanding scores its hospitals earn from the Joint Commission on Accreditation of Healthcare Organizations (JCAHO), which consistently exceed the national average.

Through two to four selective acquisitions per year, as well as continually providing services, quality, and innovation, Community Health Systems, Inc. plans to maintain its leadership in health care service delivery.

"WE BRING VALUE THROUGH OUR SIZE, EXPERIENCE, AND ADMINISTRATIVE EFFICIENCIES THAT A SMALL, INDIVIDUAL FACILITY COULD NEVER HOPE TO ACHIEVE ON ITS OWN," SAYS WAYNE SMITH, CHAIRMAN, PRESIDENT, AND CEO OF COMMUNITY HEALTH SYSTEMS, INC. HOSPITALS IN THE SYSTEM INCLUDE EASTERN NEW MEXICO MEDICAL CENTER IN ROSWELL (TOP RIGHT) AND SPRINGS MEMORIAL HOSPITAL IN LANCASTER, SOUTH CAROLINA (BOTTOM RIGHT).

Sheraton Music City Hotel

Visitors and locals alike have come to value Nashville's Sheraton Music City Hotel as something special. In a world of bustling convention hotels and take-a-number-and-wait travel destinations, the Sheraton Music City is a destination of gracious hospitality, quiet comfort, and personal attention. ◆ The 410-room hotel, designed in 1985 in the tradition of a grand southern manor,

crowns a 23-acre hilltop site off Elm Hill Pike in Century City, within easy access of the Nashville International Airport and major tourist and business destinations. Its tall, white columns, balconies, and traditional, Georgian brick exterior evoke images of Nashville's history, a graceful counterpoint to Middle Tennessee's green, rolling hills.

When guests visit the Sheraton Music City, they will discover essentially new surroundings with the same pleasant atmosphere. In January 2002, an $8 million renovation was completed that dramatically impacts all areas of the hotel. The year-long process was a renovation of all guest rooms and corridors, including new carpet, furniture, bedding, and bathrooms. The main lobby, ballrooms, and Veranda Bar have new carpet and décor.

In addition to the renovation, the hotel has added more than 4,600 square feet of meeting space from the conversion of the former Coyote Bar. This now gives the Sheraton Music City a total of 32,000 square feet of meeting space and secures the hotel's position as the second largest convention hotel in Nashville.

In a world of bustling convention hotels and take-a-number-and-wait travel destinations, the Sheraton Music City Hotel is a destination of gracious hospitality, quiet comfort, and personal attention.

THE LAP OF LUXURY

Inside, the emphasis is on quality design, luxurious amenities, and unparalleled personal service. The impressive new lobby welcomes guests with its rich, traditional colors and furnishings. The polished cherry paneling glows, and a fountain provides calming tones. Adjacent to this grand entrance, the wicker and greenery of the new Veranda Lounge invite guests to linger over a cocktail and soft piano music with friends or business associates. Nearby, the award-winning restaurant Old Hickory Grill offers Nashville's best menu of regional specialties and seasonal continental cuisine. No ordinary restaurant, Old Hickory Grill has become a favorite dining spot for discriminating locals and visitors alike.

In its new, attractive, and elegantly furnished guest rooms, the emphasis on quality and service continues. The hotel's luxurious rooms are private retreats for guests, each offering two phones, a remote control television, hair dryers, coffeemakers, irons and ironing boards, video checkout, and even video games. Every room has a spacious, private balcony, where guests can relax in comfortable chairs while enjoying a view of either the beautifully landscaped pool and courtyard or the surrounding hills.

Business travelers enjoy the 53

executive rooms and the 60 club rooms designed especially for their needs. Three presidential suites are also available. On the special Club Floor, rooms offer free local calls, voice mail and data ports, and an executive lounge where guests can enjoy a complimentary continental breakfast and hors d'oeuvres.

Parking is ample, accessible, and always complimentary. The hotel happily shuttles guests to and from Opry Mills and the airport. For recreation, the Sheraton offers its guests a fully equipped health club, massage therapy, outdoor jogging trails, and a choice of indoor and outdoor pools. The hotel is located conveniently near outstanding golf facilities.

EXTRAORDINARY SERVICE

Since it was founded, the Sheraton Music City has earned an international reputation as one of the country's finest destinations for meetings and smaller conventions, with facilities accommodating from 12 to 1,200 people. Its 32,000 square feet of beautifully decorated meeting space includes 11 small meeting rooms, a paneled executive boardroom, and the sweeping Plantation ballroom. The hotel's meeting and convention planning staff is among the best in the business, and its catering services can arrange everything from a boxed lunch to a theme buffet or a multicourse dinner with ease and attention to detail.

It is just that attention to service that has earned the Sheraton Music City 10 consecutive Gold Key awards from *Meetings and Conventions* magazine. This award, the industry's most sought after, is based on seven criteria: meetings staff, meeting rooms, guest services, food and beverage ser-

vice, reservations handling, audiovisual and other technical support equipment, and recreational facilities. The award is voted upon by the magazine's subscribers, who include corporate, incentive, and association planners– a demanding and knowledgeable group to please.

At the heart of the Sheraton Music City's success in Nashville and throughout the country is its stated mission: to be the choice of discriminating customers. The hotel achieves this goal by excelling in personal customer relations while consistently meeting the highest operational stan-

dards. Employees at the Sheraton Music City take that mission seriously and realize the crucial role they play in the hotel's success. Staff members on every level meet monthly in team planning sessions and receive ongoing professional training and education. With attention to every aspect of the business, from the friendly greetings guests receive at the door to professional appearance and efficiency in maintenance, the hotel staff strives for excellence.

Their success is measured in the Sheraton Music City's 95 percent customer satisfaction rating, setting the standard for the industry. One of only 63 corporate-managed Sheratons in North America, and the only one in Tennessee, the Sheraton Music City has also earned a place in the Sheraton Corporation's President's Club for properties with a 90-plus percent customer satisfaction rating every year since opening.

Whether visiting Nashville for fun, traveling for business, or living right here in the birthplace of country music, visitors to the Sheraton Music City Hotel feel at home in this gracious southern manor.

Since it was founded, the Sheraton Music City has earned an international reputation as one of the country's finest destinations for meetings and smaller conventions, with facilities accommodating from 12 to 1,200 people.

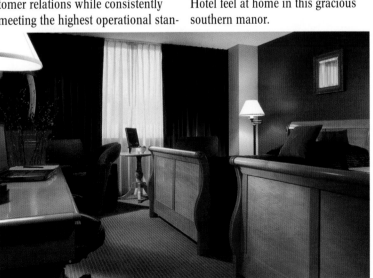

The hotel's luxurious rooms are private retreats for guests, each offering two phones, a remote control television, hair dryers, coffeemakers, irons and ironing boards, video checkout, and even video games.

Southwest Airlines

The unconventional, Dallas-based Southwest Airlines began in 1971 with a sketch on a cocktail napkin and a great deal of hope. From that humble beginning, Southwest Airlines has grown to become the fourth largest U.S. airline in terms of domestic customers carried. Year-end results for 2000 marked Southwest Airlines' 28th consecutive year of profitability. Southwest became a major airline in 1989

when it exceeded the billion-dollar revenue mark, and was the only major carrier in 1990, 1991, and 1992 to make both net and operating profits.

Southwest is the United States' only major short-haul, low-fare, high-frequency, point-to-point carrier. Southwest represents 90 percent of all the low-fare competition in the United States and consistently ranks first in market share in 80 to 90 percent of its top 100 city pairs. Southwest also carries the most passengers in the top 100 U.S. markets, despite serving only 40 of them.

Southwest provides a great deal to the communities it serves. By attracting new customers to the airport with low fares and high frequency, Southwest creates jobs for residents and revenue for the city. Southwest Airlines appeals to customers who could otherwise not afford to fly, thus increasing traffic to the airport.

Southwest Airlines entered the Nashville market in 1986, beginning with eight daily, nonstop flights to Chicago and Houston. Since then, Southwest has grown in Nashville and now operates 87 daily nonstop flights to 28 cities.

AN INDUSTRY LEADER

Southwest currently flies to 58 cities (59 airports) in 30 states and operates 2,700 flights a day. Low fares are not only a philosophical commitment at Southwest, they're essential to its short-haul market strategy. In the markets Southwest serves, ground transportation is a viable option for customers. Therefore, low fares must be charged for the company to succeed, regardless of what its air-

line competitors charge. Increased demand also is generated from charging low fares.

Many companies seek to benchmark their performance against Southwest, a company widely known as an icon for employee motivation and customer service. Southwest has also been a pioneer in the aviation industry through its many firsts. It was the first to offer profit sharing to its employees–beginning in 1973–and the first major airline to offer ticketless travel throughout its system. Southwest was the first airline to enter the information superhighway by creating its own home page on the internet and offering online booking.

AN IRREPRESSIBLE CORPORATE CULTURE

Southwest Airlines is known for its fun corporate climate created by its effervescent leader, Herb Kelleher. The chairman of the board brings charismatic leadership to his employees through antics such as arm wrestling his way out of a potential lawsuit over an advertising slogan and riding

Southwest Airlines honors its relationship with Sea World through its three Shamu 737s.

up on a Harley-Davidson at an employee party. Southwest Airlines leadership is furthered complemented by the company's chief executive officer, Jim Parker, and by Colleen Barrett, Southwest Airlines president and chief operating officer.

Most importantly, Southwest Airlines collaborates as a company to provide excellent service in every department to its customers as well as to each other. Flight attendants, wearing khaki pants and knit shirts, promote the Southwest spirit by joking with the customers and singing over the intercom during flights. When a customer is trying to reach Southwest Airlines' reservations line during peak call times, he or she will hear a humorous on-hold message to entertain and inform. Shorts and sneakers are the "uniform" for the thousands of employees who work in the airports and on flights during hot summer months. It is not unusual for a Southwest Airlines employee in any given airport to be dressed in the jersey of a local professional or college sports team. Often humorous gate and in-flight announcements set the tone for a pleasant experience on Southwest Airlines.

In terms of corporate culture, Southwest Airlines is often the yardstick for many American corporations. The airline excels in an unpredictable and unstable industry by adhering to its favorite motto: "We take the competition very seriously, but we don't take ourselves too seriously." This translates into a company whose bottom line is very disciplined, while at the same time employees are encouraged to be individuals and let their own sense of humor reflect their work style.

EMPLOYEES MAKE THE DIFFERENCE

Southwest's incomparable culture, in many ways, is the essential element that fuels the airline's growth and profitability. The company's philosophy embodies the fact that it is the employees and their personalities and dedication that make Southwest stand out in an ultra-competitive industry. Since its inception, Southwest has operated as a high-frequency, low-fare, point-to-point airline, and senior management has continued to build upon this strategy. But at the heart of any good business plan is the people who work there. Southwest has consistently emphasized individualistic, employee-driven customer service.

At Southwest, employees often cite the ability to make a difference, the so-called psychic rewards in the workplace, as the most enjoyable experience while working at Southwest. Southwest describes the recruiting process as encouraging workers to "bring your personality and your sense of humor to work."

With its emphasis on service, value, and innovation, the airline will continue to be a vital part of the Nashville area, giving its customers the freedom to fly.

Southwest Airlines is led by (from left) Jim Parker, CEO; Herb Kelleher, chairman of the board; and Colleen Barret, president and chief operating officer (left).

Promoting a fun work environment at Southwest Airlines, Kelleher joins employees at a recent bowl-a-rama (right).

Southwest Airlines gained notoriety in the 1970s by outfitting its flight attendants in hot pants.

Renaissance
Nashville Hotel

*L*ocated in the heart of downtown Nashville, the Renaissance Nashville Hotel has been providing first-class facilities and services to business and leisure travelers, convention groups, and local organizations since 1987. This AAA four-diamond convention hotel is part of the Renaissance Hotels chain managed by Marriott. Setting a new standard of excellence in luxurious accommodations, the ultramodern, 25-floor hotel features some 673 deluxe guest rooms, including 24 magnificent suites and a dramatic, four-story atrium.

SETTING THE STANDARD

The Renaissance Nashville Hotel offers a convenient business venue, and places guests in close proximity to Music City's many renowned entertainment attractions. Within walking distance of the hotel are such well-known attractions as the Second Avenue Entertainment District; the historic Ryman Auditorium; the exciting, new Country Music Hall of Fame; the breathtaking Frist Center for the Visual Arts; the Tennessee Performing Arts Center; and Riverfront Park.

After taking in the sights and sounds of Nashville, the Renaissance Nashville Hotel's guests can retreat to the comfort of the hotel, unwinding in the heated indoor pool or working out in the fully equipped fitness center. Also, guests can sample excellent cuisine and enjoy the stunning view of the cityscape from the hotel's restaurants and lounges–Commerce Street Grille, the Bridge Lounge & Deli, or Lobbies Bar.

Just 15 minutes from Nashville International Airport, the Renaissance provides a number of services and amenities designed to surround guests in comfort. The top two floors are exclusive Renaissance Club levels with private-key access, and feature an elegant private lounge and concierge service, as well as complimentary continental breakfast Monday through Friday and evening hors d'oeuvres every Sunday through Thursday.

All of the hotel's spacious guest rooms are beautifully appointed, and offer amenities such as coffeemakers, in-room movies and video games, irons and ironing boards, cable television, computer dataports, and no surcharge on toll-free and credit card calls up to 20 minutes. Guests can also take advantage of the Downtown Airport Express™, which provides regularly scheduled shuttle service to Nashville International Airport.

IDEAL VENUE FOR MEETINGS AND EVENTS

A first-class hotel for hosting conventions and meetings, the Renaissance Nashville has been honored with many awards, including *Successful Meetings'* Pinnacle Award, as well as being cited on *Facilities* magazine's list of elite hotels.

The hotel connects to the Nashville Convention Center and the 20,000-seat Gaylord Entertainment Center, affording groups a total of 205,000 square feet of meeting space–the most in downtown Nashville. The complex features a 119,000-square-foot exhibition hall, 18,000- and 11,000-square-foot ballrooms, and 45 additional meeting rooms. An outstanding team of culinary, banquet, and audiovisual professionals attends to each and every detail to ensure a successful event.

The Renaissance Nashville Hotel truly provides the best Music City has to offer. Its exceptional meeting and convention facilities, elegant accommodations, and refined personal service, as well as its convenient proximity to downtown business and entertainment, keep guests coming back time and again.

Located in the heart of downtown Nashville, the Renaissance Nashville Hotel has been providing first-class facilities and services to business and leisure travelers, convention groups, and local organizations since 1987.

Nashville

Visitors to Middle Tennessee are struck time and again by the region's abundant natural beauty. Its rolling hills, sparkling streams, and diverse wildlife make it a natural draw for hikers, photographers, paddlers, anglers, and those who just need to get away from it all. Showcasing this beauty and Tennessee's rich cultural history are Tennessee's state parks, which are managed

by the Tennessee Department of Environment and Conservation (TDEC).

TDEC was created in 1991 when the Department of Health and Environment and the Department of Conservation were reorganized to create the Department of Environment and Conservation, an effort to comprehensively protect and conserve Tennessee's environment and unique natural and cultural resources. TDEC is headquartered in Nashville with eight regional offices across the state. The organization's biologists, engineers, and other environmental experts work to keep Tennessee beautiful by closely regulating and monitoring the quality of the state's air, land, and water.

PREMIER RESORT PARKS

Visitors to Nashville and surrounding communities are just a short drive away from one of Tennessee's 54 magnificent state parks. The park system offers diverse recreational opportunities for individuals, families, businesses, and professional groups, from a scenic hike in a pristine natural area to a round of championship golf.

Less than an hour west of Nashville is one of Tennessee's premier resort parks, Montgomery Bell State Resort Park. The park is home to a new restaurant and inn with 110 rooms, five suites, a glass-enclosed indoor pool, a jacuzzi, and an outdoor pool—all overlooking beautiful Lake Acorn. The park has a new conference center with more than 6,000 square feet of meeting space, banquet service, and a state-of-the-art sound system, making it the natural choice for a business conference.

South of Nashville lies Tims Ford State Park, an anglers' paradise. The park's 10,700-acre Tims Ford Lake

is one of the most picturesque in Tennessee and is regarded as one of the top bass fishing and recreational lakes in the Southeast. The park's championship golf course and modern, spacious cabins make it the perfect spot for a family vacation or a corporate retreat.

RECYCLING PROGRAMS

Tennessee state parks are also setting a good example when it comes to recycling. Just about everyone knows that recycling saves landfill space and energy. What many don't know is that recy-

cling also saves taxpayers' dollars by reducing the cost of waste disposal at state parks.

Radnor Lake State Natural Area and Paris Landing State Park have had active recycling programs for years. Tim's Ford State Park, Pinson Mounds Archeological Area, and T.O. Fuller State Park kicked off successful recycling programs in 2001. "We wanted to set a good example for our visitors," says Environment and Conservation Commissioner Milton Hamilton. "We hope people will learn about recycling while visiting our parks, and make it a habit when they return home."

A park ranger does his part to preserve the environment by recycling at Tims Ford State Park.

Bicentennial Mall State Park in downtown Nashville showcases Tennessee history and provides a great learning experience for children and adults alike (left).

Just a short drive from the hustle and bustle of Nashville, the 1,100-acre Radnor Lake State Natural Area provides a refuge for wildlife and the perfect spot for a relaxing walk in the woods (right).

Airport Ramada Inn & Suites

The friendly greeting at the front desk sets the tone for a guest's stay at the Airport Ramada Inn & Suites. Obliging employees, a convenient location, and the comforts of home are hallmarks of this all-suite property–the only all-suite Ramada in Nashville, which opened in 1988. ◆ Having received Ramada's esteemed Gold Key status, a quality designation achieved by only 323

other properties in the large Ramada system, the Ramada Inn & Suites takes pride in its personnel, cleanliness, aesthetics, meal service, and overall maintenance.

In addition to Ramada Inn & Suites' attention to detail, guests appreciate its proximity to the airport, downtown, and favorite tourist attractions. Just a few miles from the airport and the Opry Mills shopping and entertainment complex, and six miles from downtown, the Ramada can truly boast location, location, location. For those getting married at the quaint Bridal Path Wedding Chapel next door, Ramada Inn & Suites serves as a convenient and luxurious choice for their reception and stay.

PERSONAL BEST

While signs in the lobby explain Ramada's corporate Personal Best Hospitality philosophy, the hotel's commitment is clearly seen through its professional staff. Personal Best is about attitude–having the determination to do one's personal best to care for guests and ensure a memorable experience.

The cordial staff strives to make everyone feel at home. Management has an open-door policy in an effort to be available for any question or concern by the guest. And all employees try to keep abreast of Music City happenings. Whether providing directions, recommending a restaurant or suggest-ing an entertainment venue for the night, the staff always puts forward its personal best.

The hotel and staff also exude community pride and spirit. They take an active role in supporting local schools–giving door prizes of complimentary room nights for school festivals or volunteering time to help schools and students in need.

Corporately, Ramada does its best to help care for the needy children of

The Airport Ramada Inn & Suites is just a few miles from the airport and the Opry Mills shopping and entertainment complex, and six miles from downtown.

the world. Ramada is committed to the work of Childreach, the U.S. member of PLAN International, one of the largest humanitarian organizations in the world. Childreach's field programs are tailor-made to help each sponsored child and family meet basic needs, improve their conditions and rise out of desperate circumstances. As a sponsor itself, Ramada in turn encourages guests to become Childreach sponsors. Brochures explaining the exceptional work of the Childreach program and how others can help are available in the Ramada lobby.

ALL SUITES, ALL THE TIME

The moderately priced property is attractive to both leisure and corporate travelers. Its diverse settings comfortably accommodate families, couples traveling together, and those traveling on business to Nashville for extended periods of time. A total of 120 studio and one- and two-bedroom suites are available, each offering a full-size kitchen and separate sleeping area. The one- and two-bedroom suites also offer a living room. In-room amenities include cable television, complimentary Showtime,

data port, voice mail, and coffee. Guests can relax by the outdoor pool or in the heated spa. Ramada also provides its guests with a complimentary deluxe continental breakfast each morning in the atrium and complimentary shuttles to the airport, and can provide transportation to nearby restaurants and Opry Mills Mall. Additional services include dry cleaning valet, onsite laundry facilities, pay per view movies, safety deposit boxes, and fax and copy services.

Small groups also take advantage of the Ramada Inn & Suites' conference and banquet facilities. The Ramada offers three rooms ranging in size from 228 square feet to more than 1,000 square feet. The Nashville Room is ideally suited for intimate board meetings or small conferences. The Tennessee Room can seat 75 people and is equipped with a full kitchen and restroom facilities. Perfect for meal functions, socials, and smaller meetings, the attractive atrium is naturally lit and looks out to the swimming pool and courtyard. Extensive audio-visual capabilities as well as high-speed Internet service are available in all rooms as needed. Handicap facilities are also available. And all guests–whether attending for business or pleasure–appreciate complimentary parking.

The Ramada Inn & Suites makes it easy for guests to book rooms via its Web site at ramadainnnashville.com, where they can find information and make reservations. Through the Club Rewards and Senior Savers programs, guests can accrue points every time they stay at a Ramada location and redeem them for free stays and vacations at Ramada. But warm smiles, obliging dispositions, gracious accommodations, and a stellar location are incentive enough to return to the Airport Ramada Inn & Suites in Nashville.

A total of 120 studio and one- and two-bedroom suites are available, each offering a full-size kitchen and separate sleeping area.

Small groups also take advantage of the Ramada Inn & Suites' conference and banquet facilities. The Ramada offers three rooms ranging in size from 228 square feet to more than 1,000 square feet.

Curb Records Inc.

Mike Curb could be called "the power behind the tone." He has built Curb Records Inc. into one of the most successful independent record labels in the United States. Curb has a 35-year track record of working with pop and country music stars such as Sammy Davis Jr., Hank Williams Jr., the Osmonds, Lou Rawls, Lyle Lovett, LeAnn Rimes,

Tim McGraw, Jo Dee Messina, and the Judds.

Curb–songwriter, producer, and record company owner–launched and built his career in Los Angeles, but with an interest in country music, knew he should be in Nashville. In 1992, Curb Records moved its corporate headquarters and top executives to Nashville's illustrious Music Row.

MOVING TO MUSIC CITY

At the time of the move, Nashville was experiencing the early stages of explosive growth in the country music industry. Curb recognized that in order to be successful in the country music arena, his company needed to be in Nashville.

Beginning in 1993, the label started to see success with such artists as McGraw, Hal Ketchum, Sawyer Brown, and Wynonna Judd. That same year, Curb

Records tapped into the pop music industry, bringing back the Righteous Brothers' "Unchained Melody," and releasing "December 1963 (Oh What a Night)" by the Four Seasons.

In mid-1994, the company decided to expand its presence in country music, forming a second Curb label, which signed artists Junior Brown, Williams, Jeff Carson, and Rimes. In the late 1990s, Curb Records also ventured into contemporary Christian music, signing such artists as Jonathan Pierce

and Selah. "The new venture made sense because it fit the personality of the company and the geography–it was all happening in Nashville," says Curb.

By the end of 1997, *Soundscan* had recognized the Curb group of labels as the largest in Nashville–no small feat for an independent record company in Music City. In 1998, the company won four *Billboard* awards for top single, top album, top country album, and top Christian album.

Curb Records Inc. has worked with such internationally known country artists as (top row, from left) Hal Ketchum, Hank Williams Jr., (middle row, from left) Lyle Lovett, Tim McGraw, Junior Brown, (bottom row, from left) Sawyer Brown, Wynonna, and LeAnn Rimes.

INDEPENDENCE BREEDS SUCCESS

But for Curb, success lies far beyond the revenues generated by the company. Curb takes pride in how his company operates within the industry, with a long-term view and commitment toward its artists and employees.

"We correlate a lot of our success to our move to Tennessee," says Curb. "In a difficult business that demands a lot of creativity, Nashville has the ambience that allows for that state of mind. Everything from lifestyle to employees being happier raising their families has been terrific."

The company's biggest endeavor in the community has been the founding and funding of the Curb School of Music Business at Belmont University in Nashville. "The program has become so large at Belmont that it is now operating as a separate school," says Curb. "We are very proud of this effort."

Being independent, Curb Records also attributes its success to its ability to move very quickly in the marketplace, discovering and signing artists, as well as adapting to a volatile industry with regard to promotions and advertising. "That freedom allows us to do things that are directly responsible for the success we've had over the years," says Curb.

A 35-YEAR TRACK RECORD

Curb began his exceptional career in the mid-1960s at age 18, when he began releasing soundtrack albums he composed for motion pictures. His own group, the Mike Curb Congregation, appeared weekly on national television as part of the *Glen Campbell Show* on CBS, and recorded number one hit records such as "Candy Man" with Sammy Davis Jr. and "Burning Bridges" from the Clint Eastwood movie *Kelly's Heroes*.

In 1969, Curb merged his company with MGM Records and became president of the new venture. During his tenure, Curb turned out hits like "One Bad Apple" by the Osmonds, Lou Rawls' "Natural Man," and "I'm Leaving It All Up to You" by Donny and Marie Osmond.

When MGM was sold in 1974, Curb went on to build the Curb Music Company and the Curb/Warner label. At one time, the company had five number one songs on the chart, including Debby Boone's "You Light Up My Life," the biggest-selling record of the decade.

The Curb group of labels, with offices in Los Angeles and Nashville, encompasses a variety of music. Curb works on both coasts as he continues to produce movie soundtracks as he did when he launched his career. In 2000, the label released the soundtrack for Disney's *Coyote Ugly*, which became a number one seller, and for Warner Brothers' *Driven*. Curb confirms that the emphasis for today and the future of his company is on country music.

Curb maintains that Curb Records' major contribution to the music industry is in its success with signing, recording, and bringing artists to the marketplace who may not have otherwise had their music presented. "We are very bullish on the music industry in the coming years, and see Nashville as continuing to be more of a linchpin in terms of all music," says Curb. "The city will become an entertainment center. However, Nashville will always remain a mecca for country music."

XO Communications, Inc.

Following the deregulation of the telecommunications industry, XO Communications, Inc. officially opened in Nashville on July 4, 1996, with a mission to offer business customers a choice from their traditional telephone providers. ◆ Empowered by a David versus Goliath mentality, XO™ started small, taking one strategic step at a time. While other start-ups

rushed into new markets by simply reselling existing lines, XO quietly built its own network around the community. Your Phone Service Redefined was the company's original tagline as it assured customers they would no longer be "over-promised and under-served." XO embraced its first customers who, like XO, were telecommunications pioneers in the post-Bell era.

A GROWING FOOTPRINT

Craig McCaw founded XO in Seattle in 1994 to provide high-quality broadband communications services to businesses over fiber-optic facilities. Currently, XO holds the largest fixed wireless spectrum in North America, with li-

censes covering 95 percent of the population in the top 30 U.S. markets. XO currently offers facilities-based broadband communications services in more than 60 markets throughout the United States.

The company's broadband wireless capabilities complement and extend the reach of XO local fiber-optic networks. Unlike traditional telecommunications networks, the XO long-haul and metro networks are fiber optic, meaning transmissions are sent as light pulses rather than electric signals, resulting in a more reliable network with greater potential transmission capacity than an electrical network.

Equipped with this growing footprint of facilities it owns, along with

multiple broadband access technologies, XO provides quality broadband services that can open the last, or "golden," mile bottleneck, which has frustrated the realization of true high-speed communications. The XO network is already one of the first truly integrated U.S. telecommunications systems capable of supporting both voice and data transmissions.

NOT JUST TALK

Nashville was one of the initial launch cities for XO. "Our employees had to work long hours to make this company a success. But we took pride in building a 'family-like' corporate culture," says Jim Price, area vice president for the XO southern

XO Communications, Inc. currently offers facilities-based broadband communications services in more than 60 markets throughout the United States.

While other start-ups rushed into new markets by simply reselling existing lines, XO quietly built its own network around the community.

region. "Nobody else had done what we did. We were building on innovation from the beginning in how we served customers, established pricing, and the like."

The company launched its Nashville office with a handful of employees and today has more than 500 working from its downtown headquarters. In a move that reflects the unique XO corporate culture, the office itself was designed by employees and features modern, curved, and open workspaces.

In fall 2000, the company then known as NEXTLINK merged with Concentric, a data services company, which together became XO Communications. As services expanded beyond telecommunications and into data and broadband, XO adopted a new tagline: Not Just Talk.

The double entendre of its tagline reinforces the company's promise. "Customer care is big for us," says Price. "One of our core values is to exceed customers' expectations. We work hard to anticipate their needs and proactively care for them."

XO can be more responsive to customer needs because it owns and controls its own network. Its state-of-the-art network is located in the same downtown Nashville building where all its employees work. Because the company owns its network and is close to it, repair times are reduced. The company also provides a 24-hour customer care center.

"Our customers find that they have a person to talk to locally if they have a problem with their service, and that's reassuring," says Price. "Additionally, our customers like the ease of receiving one bill with their local, long distance, and Internet charges all together. Ultimately, we are able to offer a better service level and more robust products at highly competitive rates." XO business services run the gamut from local and long distance voice services, digital subscriber line, and Internet access to virtual private networks, Web hosting, e-commerce, and private data networking services.

Befitting its entrepreneurial spirit—and a first for the industry—XO introduced its first bundled services program, XOptions™. Customers have the option to pay a flat monthly rate for its voice, data, and Web services.

INVESTING IN RELATIONSHIPS

XO has tackled community work in Nashville with the same zeal as it showed between 1996 and 2001 in launching its network. For example, XO partnered with WWTN radio to support the Charles Davis Shootout, a popular fund-raiser that benefits underprivileged kids.

"We believe in sharing the experience and not just writing a check," says Price. "We set up and manned a phone bank at our offices to generate pledges. We've gotten our customers involved, matched their pledges, and our employees help staff the event."

Recognizing that its success is contingent upon its customers' success, the company dedicates itself to creating opportunities to help grow its customers' business. As the company grows throughout the 21st century with an unrivaled collection of facilities, XO Communications, Inc. aims to deliver innovative telecommunications solutions for all its customers.

Citadel Communications Corporation

itadel Communications Corporation serves the Nashville community in radio broadcasting as a host of stations known for integrity and quality service. Based in Las Vegas, Nevada, Citadel owns more than 200 stations nationwide, and joined the Nashville business community in 2000 with the acquisition of WKDF-FM (103.3) and WGFX-FM (104.5). ◆ WKDF became part

of Nashville's radio lore when the 30-year-old rock music station aired its last song, "End of the World" by REM. The legendary force in rock music had moved to an alternative format before switching to country. Alan Jackson's "Don't Rock the Jukebox" was the first song played under the new format, signaling a new era for the radio station.

The station enjoyed much of its rock-oriented success under the ownership of Dick Broadcasting Company in Knoxville. Dick Broadcasting acquired WKDA-AM, another fabled Nashville station, and WKDF in July 1976. WKDA had been on the air since December 1946 and originally featured live music, news, and local sports, including the Nashville Vols baseball games. From 1956 to 1970, WKDA programmed a Top 40 format and dominated the Nashville market from its broadcast studios atop the 12th floor of the downtown Stahlman Building. In 1970, WKDA changed its format to country and was later sold by Dick Broadcasting in 1995.

THE MAKING OF A RADIO LEGEND

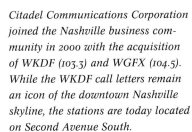

Citadel Communications Corporation joined the Nashville business community in 2000 with the acquisition of WKDF (103.3) and WGFX (104.5). While the WKDF call letters remain an icon of the downtown Nashville skyline, the stations are today located on Second Avenue South.

WKDF originally went on the air as WNFO-FM in April 1962 with 16,700 watts. Its programming was a surprising array of mainstream album tracking, country, religion, and even a Hawaiian music block at night. The Hawaiian music gave way to more sports programming, which included the broadcast of Father Ryan High School football and the Dixie Flyers hockey team. WNFO was taken off the air in June 1966 in order to move to its new studios in the Stahlman Building, joining its then sister station WKDA. The station returned to the airwaves in 1967 on the FM dial,

playing an automated middle-of-the-road format. A gradual programming change to progressive rock occurred as the station increased its power to 100,000 watts. Shortly before Dick Broadcasting purchased the station in 1976, the station began programming album-oriented rock. After the purchase, the new owners changed the call letters to WKDF, moved the studios to Second Avenue South, and achieved long-standing success as Nashville's pure rock-and-roll station. The W on the Stahlman building sign was turned off to reflect the popular reference to the station as simply KDF.

Owned since the mid-1970s by

Dick Broadcasting, the stations had been insulated from the mass buyouts many of its competitors were experiencing in the 1990s by large broadcast corporations. However, change is inevitable in any business, and in October 2000, WKDF and WGFX were among Dick Broadcasting properties sold to Citadel Communications. The transition has been smooth as longtime managers and staffers remained in place, conducting business as usual and continuing a tradition of leadership and community spirit. According to 30-year employee and General Manager Steve Dickert, "The Citadel model is not unlike the Dick

Broadcasting tradition of believing in its people and giving them the tools they need to achieve respect and excellence in their field."

Citadel Communications, led by Chairman and CEO Larry Wilson, completed an initial public offering of common stock in 1998. Citadel itself was acquired by Forstmann Little & Company in June 2001, but still maintains day-to-day management of its stations.

CARL P. AND THE P-TEAM

Anchoring WKDF in the morning is the award-winning air personality Carl P. Mayfield. Consistently recognized as one of the nation's top radio personalities, Mayfield cemented his radio career at WKDF during the rock years from 1970 to 1990. Headlines were made in the early 1990s when Mayfield left the station briefly to explore his country side. Mayfield made headlines again when he rejoined WKDF on April 1, 1999, with the unveiling of the new country format station, Music City 103.

Despite those who were convinced it was an April Fools' Day joke, WKDF has climbed the ranks since then to rival Nashville's other country stations. Mayfield and his comrades spin today's new country hits, as well as music from country's all-time legends. Listeners tune in to hear the latest hits from the Dixie Chicks, Garth Brooks, Faith Hill, Tim McGraw, George Strait, and Martina McBride, as well as the legends such as George Jones, Merle Haggard, Waylon Jennings, and Loretta Lynn.

Mayfield has debuted new music on his show, including the world radio premier of the Country Music

Association's award-winning "Murder on Music Row" by Alan Jackson and George Strait and the more recent "Riding with Private Malone" by David Ball, a song about a Vietnam veteran that touched the hearts of listeners moved to patriotism by the terrible events of September 11, 2001. Mayfield's show also features his weekly Waylon Wednesday interviews with country legend Waylon Jennings.

Joining Mayfield each morning from 6 a.m. to 10 a.m. are P-Team members news sidekick Mike "the Duke of News" Donegan, sportsman Mark "the Shark" Howard, the P-Team Gals Jeana Leyhew (executive producer) and Britt Savage, Luke "the Drifter" Williams, and Jeff Lyon. The fun gets cranked up by Mayfield's popular alter egos: Freebird Trailer Park buddy Bubba Skynyrd; Brother Jonah, the miracle household appliance healer from the Loose Change Country Cathedral; Peanut, owner of Peanut's All-American Auto Parts; and Homeless Jimmy, Nashville's lovable panhandler. Bubba Skynyrd once held the radio station hostage

for 24 hours, playing "Freebird" back-to-back and gleefully making headlines in the local papers. Bubba, never one to be bashful about his politics, also ran twice for mayor and once for sheriff, challenging longtime incumbent Fate Thomas to a debate on the roof of the radio station. Bubba lost the vote but won the hearts of the people.

Mayfield has received a host of national awards and honors. In 1994, he was awarded the Country Music Association's coveted CMA Air Personality of the Year award. Mayfield has also been nominated for the National Association of Broadcasters' Marconi Award in the category of Large Market Air Personality. He has been named *Billboard* magazine's Air Personality of the Year as well, and in May 2001 was named the Academy of Country Music's DJ of the Year. In addition, Mayfield has been a guest on *Good Morning America* and *Entertainment Tonight.*

Mayfield is followed by a talented crew of on-air personalities, including 36-year radio veteran C.C. McCartney, who was nominated for Best Radio

The WKDF morning show's P-Team includes (top, from left) Luke Williams, Jeff Lyon, (bottom, from left) Jeana Leyhew, Mike Donegan, Carl P. Mayfield, Mark Howard, and Britt Savage.

The fun at WKDF gets cranked up by Mayfield's popular alter egos, most notably his buddy Bubba Skynyrd. Skynyrd, never one to be bashful about his politics, ran twice for mayor and once for sheriff, challenging longtime incumbent Fate Thomas to a debate on the roof of the radio station (left).

Mayfield is pictured here with (from left) Waylon Jennings, George Jones, and Alan Jackson (right).

In September 1999, Mayfield (bottom right) launched an event that is now known as Rolling Titan Thunder. To commemorate the Tennessee Titans first regular season game at Adelphia Coliseum, Mayfield invited friends such as Waylon Jennings (top right) to help with a charity motorcycle ride and concert. The event has grown each year, with Alan Jackson (top left, pictured with wife Denise) serving as grand marshal in 2000 and 2001.

Personality by the CMA four times. McCartney has also hosted syndicated radio programs such as *Climbing Country*, *The Back Forty*, and *Starline*. Eddie Fox and his sidekick producer Stunt Boy Justin bring irrepressible humor and crazy antics to the airwaves, having been thrown in jail, suspended by giant cranes, and stranded on billboards.

GIVING BACK TO THE COMMUNITY

When approached by the mother of Blaine Neltnor, a young boy dying of liver disease, Mayfield began a relentless drive and raised enough money for a transplant for Neltnor and another baby, John Frazier, also in need of a livesaving liver transplant. Both boys are now teenagers living life to the fullest.

Committed to the community, Mayfield has spearheaded WKDF's massive community fund-raisers, such as the popular One for the Sun concerts, featuring local and nationally known artists. He has held charity golf tournaments, inviting many of his celebrity friends to tee off at various local courses. These annual events and others funded WKDF's Rock for Toys, which provided new toys for 103 needy children at Christmas, and other child-related concerns. The fund-raisers continue with Mayfield, a Vietnam veteran, appealing to listeners to help bring the traveling replica of

the Vietnam Veteran's Memorial to Nashville's Bicentennial Park on an annual basis, beginning in May 2001, for Armed Services Day.

In September 1999, Mayfield launched an event that is now known as Rolling Titan Thunder. To commemorate the Tennessee Titans first regular season game at Adelphia Coliseum, Mayfield invited friends such as Waylon Jennings and Travis Tritt to help with a charity motorcycle ride and concert. The event has grown each year, with Alan Jackson serving as grand marshal in 2000 and 2001 and Ronnie Milsap headlining the 2000 concert. In September 2001, more than 2,500 motorcycles roared around the new Nashville Superspeedway in three memorial laps to the late Dale Earnhardt, then thundered 40 miles to downtown Nashville and circled Adelphia Coliseum before arriving at Riverfront Park to kick off a concert headlined by Hank Williams Jr.

Rolling Titan Thunder has raised tens of thousands of dollars for the Chris Sanders Foundation and Operation Stand Down.

104 THE CORE

By the time Citadel Communications purchased WGFX in May 2000, the FM station had gone through an alphabet soup of call letters, monikers, owners, and formats. The station originally went on the air in 1960 as WFMG. In 1972, the call letters changed to WIHN, and by the end of the decade, the call letters had changed to WWKX Kicks 104 with a Top 40 format. Capitol Broadcasting acquired the license in 1986, and by August 1987, after playing "Kicks" by Paul Revere & the Raiders nonstop for an hour, Kicks 104 faded off the air and WGFX 104 the Fox was born.

Originally billed as a "classic hits station" the first song played on the

Fox was "Layla" by Derick and the Dominoes. The station quickly evolved into Nashville's premier classic rock station. In 1991, the station was sold to HaPa Inc., and a lease management agreement was inked with Dick Broadcasting's WKDA/WKDF. In September 1992, an application for ownership was filed with the FCC, and Nashville's first FM duopoly was formed. The WGFX studios were then consolidated with WKDA/WKDF.

In January 1994, WGFX introduced a new oldies format. The station changed its name to Groovin' Hits 104.5 before going back to its classic rock roots as today's 104 the Core.

Designed to reach baby boomers who grew up during the 1970s, WGFX plays classic rock from the mid-1960s through the 1980s. One of the hottest formats on radio, the playlist includes Eric Clapton, Doobie Brothers, the Eagles, Led Zeppelin, Fleetwood Mac, and Bob Seger. Mornings at the Core are kicked off by the syndicated Rick 'n' Bubba, the hilarious "two sexiest fat men alive," followed by great classic rock to get listeners through the day.

TITANS RADIO NETWORK

WGFX serves as the official flagship station of Titans Radio, the Tennessee Titans radio network, providing year-round coverage for the 1999 AFC Champion Tennessee Titans. WGFX has been the home of pro football since 1996, when Titans Owner Bud Adams announced he would move the Oilers to Nashville and a new home on the banks of the Cumberland River.

From the first moments of Eddie George's record-setting 216-yard rushing day in Memphis back in 1997 to the unveiling of Adelphia Coliseum in August 1999, from the Titans comeback in Superbowl XXXIV to all the special moments of the team's 13-3 season in 2000, WGFX has been on the air with the award-winning play-by-play of the NFL's most outstanding broadcast network.

The most memorable moment for Titans Radio came in January 2000 when the Voice of the Titans Mike Keith and color analyst Pat Ryan made history with their description of the Titans playoff win over Buffalo in Nashville. Ryan's announcement that "he's got something" echoed on WGFX and on the more than 65 stations nationwide as the Titans pulled out a 22-16 playoff win over Buffalo. As Kevin Dyson scored the go-ahead touchdown, Keith called it a miracle, and the name Music City Miracle as well as the Titans Radio call are synonymous with the play.

WGFX serves as the official flagship station of Titans Radio, the Tennessee Titans radio network, providing year-round coverage for the 1999 AFC Champion Tennessee Titans. Mike Keith (right) serves as the Voice of the Titans.

Towery Publishing

Beginning as a small publisher of local newspapers in 1935, Towery Publishing, a division of Baretz Publishing, LLC, today has become a global publisher of a diverse range of community-based materials from San Diego to Sydney. Its products—such as the company's award-winning Urban Tapestry Series, business

directories, magazines, and Internet sites—continue to build on Towery's distinguished heritage of excellence, making its name synonymous with service, utility, and quality.

COMMUNITY PUBLISHING AT ITS BEST

Towery Publishing has long been the industry leader in community-based publications. In 1972, current President J. Robert Towery succeeded his parents in managing the printing and publishing business they had founded four decades earlier. "One of the more impressive traits of my family's publishing business was its dedication to presenting only the highest quality products available—whatever our market might be," says Towery. "Since taking over the company, I've continued our fight for the high ground in maintaining this tradition."

During the 1970s and 1980s, Towery expanded the scope of the company's published materials to include *Memphis* magazine and other successful regional and national publications, such as *Memphis Shopper's Guide, Racquetball* magazine, *Huddle/*

FastBreak, Real Estate News, and *Satellite Dish* magazine. In 1985, after selling its locally focused assets, the company began the trajectory on which it continues today, creating community-oriented materials that are often produced in conjunction with chambers of commerce and other business organizations.

All of Towery Publishing's efforts, represented on the Internet at www.towery.com, are marked by a careful, innovative design philosophy that has become a hallmark of the company's reputation for quality and service. Boasting a nationwide sales force, proven editorial depth, cutting-edge graphic capabilities, ample sales and marketing resources, and extensive data management expertise, the company has assembled the intellectual and capital resources necessary to produce quality products and services.

In 2001, Towery became a wholly owned subsidiary of The Oxford Companies of Chicago. Oxford, which employs some 7,000 people, makes equity investments for itself and its investors, and owns companies in health care, commercial finance, telephone, and publishing industries.

URBAN TAPESTRY SERIES

Towery Publishing launched its popular Urban Tapestry Series in 1990. Each of the nearly 100 oversized, hardbound photojournals details the people, history, culture, environment, and commerce of a featured metropolitan area. These colorful coffee-table books spotlight communities through an introductory essay authored by a noted local individual, an exquisite collection of photographs, and in-depth profiles of select companies and organizations that form the area's business core.

From New York to Vancouver to Los Angeles, national and international authors have graced the pages of the books' introductory essays. The celebrated list of contributors includes two former U.S. presidents—Gerald Ford (Grand Rapids) and Jimmy Carter (Atlanta); boxing great Muhammad Ali (Louisville); two network newscasters—CBS anchor Dan Rather (Austin) and ABC anchor Hugh Downs (Phoenix); NBC sportscaster Bob Costas (St. Louis); record-breaking quarterback Steve Young (San Francisco); best-selling mystery author Robert B. Parker (Boston); American

Towery Publishing President J. Robert Towery (left) took the reins of his family's business in 1972, maintaining the company's long-standing core commitment to quality.

Nashville

Sorting through hundreds of beautiful photographs is just one of the enviable tasks assigned to Towery's top-notch team of designers and art directors, led by award-winning Creative Director Brian Groppe (left). Members of Towery's editorial staff cull the best from materials submitted by feature writers and profile clients to produce the Urban Tapestry Series (right).

Movie Classics host Nick Clooney (Cincinnati); former Texas first lady Nellie Connally (Houston); and former New York City Mayor Ed Koch (New York).

While the books have been enormously successful, the company continues to improve and redefine the role the series plays in the marketplace. "Currently, the Urban Tapestry Series works beautifully as a tool for enhancing the image of the communities it portrays," says Towery. "As the series continues to mature, we want it to become a reference source that businesses and executives turn to when evaluating the quality of life in cities where they may be considering moving or expanding."

CHAMBERS OF COMMERCE TURN TO TOWERY

In addition to its Urban Tapestry Series, Towery Publishing has become the largest producer of published and Internet materials for North American chambers of commerce. From published membership directories and Internet listings that enhance business-to-business communication, to visitor and relocation guides tailored to reflect the unique qualities of the communities they cover, the company's chamber-oriented materials offer comprehensive information on dozens of topics, including housing, education, leisure activities, health care, and local government.

The company's primary Internet product consists of its introCity™ sites. Much like its published materials, Towery's introCity sites introduce newcomers, visitors, and longtime residents to every facet of a particular community, while simultaneously

placing the local chamber of commerce at the forefront of the city's Internet activity. The sites provide newcomer information including calendars, photos, citywide business listings with everything from nightlife to shopping to family fun, and on-line maps pinpointing the exact location of businesses, schools, attractions, and much more.

SUSTAINED CREATIVITY

The driving forces behind Towery Publishing have always been the company's employees and its state-of-the-art industry technology. Many of its employees have worked with the Towery family of companies for more than 20 years. Today's staff of seasoned innovators totals around 100 at the Memphis headquarters, and more than 40 sales, marketing, and editorial staff traveling to and working in an ever growing list of cities.

Supporting the staff's endeavors is state-of-the-art prepress publishing software and equipment. Towery Publishing was the first production environment in the United States to combine desktop publishing with color separations and image scanning to produce finished film suitable for burning plates for four-color printing. Today, the company relies on its digital prepress services to produce more than 8,000 pages each year, containing more than 30,000 high-quality color images.

Through decades of business and technological change, one aspect of Towery Publishing has remained constant. "The creative energies of our staff drive us toward innovation and invention," Towery says. "Our people make the highest possible demands on themselves, so I know that our future is secure if the ingredients for success remain a focus on service and quality."

With The Open Container—an outdoor sculpture by Memphian Mark Nowell—marking the spot, Towery's Memphis home office serves as the headquarters for the company's innovative, community-based publications.

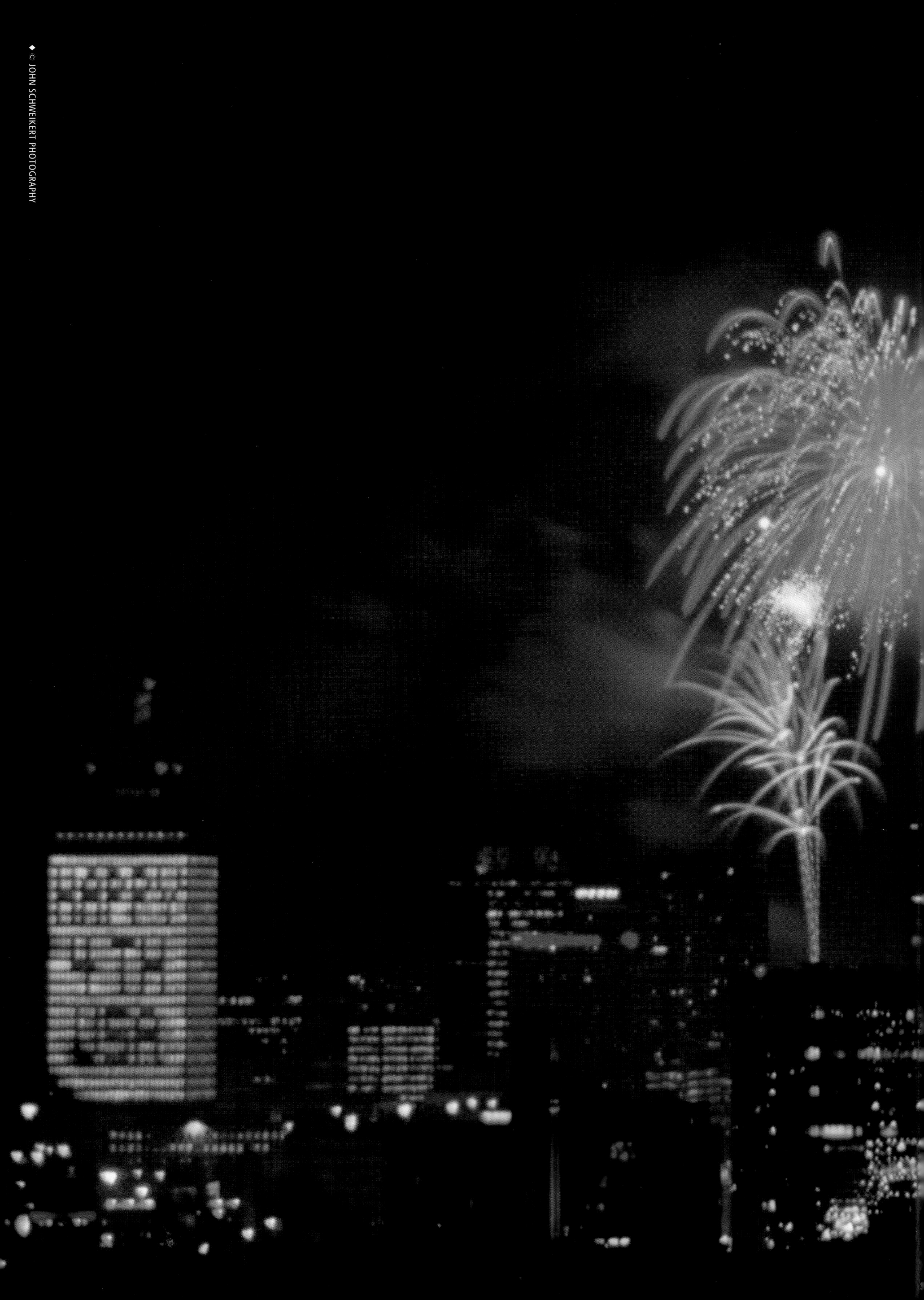

© JOHN SCHWEIKERT PHOTOGRAPHY

Photographers

STEVE BAKER is an international photographer who has contributed to more than 100 publications. As the proprietor of Highlight Photography, he specializes in assignments for clients such as Eastman Kodak, Nike, Budweiser, the U.S. Olympic Committee, and Mobil Oil, which has commissioned seven exhibitions of his work since 1994. Baker is author and photographer of *Racing Is Everything*, and has contributed to numerous other Towery publications.

Owner of Boehm Photographic, **SCOTT BOEHM** specializes in photography and graphic design. His images document various sporting events around the country.

NEIL J. BRAKE is the chief photographer of the Public Affairs Department at Vanderbilt University, and concentrates on photojournalism, sports photography, and spot news. His coverage of Alabama Coach "Bear" Bryant's last game at the Liberty Bowl earned him almost complete photographic representation for the following day's edition of the *Birmingham News* in Alabama, and he has had various images published in *Sports Illustrated*, *Time*, *Newsweek*, and the *New York Times*.

With 12 years' experience as a photojournalist, **MICHAEL CLANCY** has had images published in the *Baltimore Sun*, *Rocky Mountain News*, *Tennessean*, and *Los Angeles Times*. He has won 14 Picture of the Year awards from the Tennessee Press Association, and his image *Fetal Hand Grasp* has been published in magazines and newspapers around the world.

With a broad range of people, nature, architecture, and technology imagery to his credit, **DAVID A. DOBBS** operates Dobbs Photography, where he focuses on corporate, editorial, and stock photography. His work has appeared in *National Geographic Explorer*, *U.S. News & World Report*, and *Life*, as well as in several other Towery publications.

LEE FOSTER, a veteran travel writer and photographer, has had work published in major travel magazines and newspapers. He maintains a stock library that features images of more than 250 destinations around the world.

Originally from Kentucky, **WINDLE C. HARMON** concentrates on landscape photography for Aerostructures Corp. He has attended photography classes at Nashville Tech, and won Honorable Mention awards from *Popular Photography* for his nature images.

A contributing editor to *Vacations* and *Cruises & Tours* magazines, and coauthor of the travel guidebook *Hidden Coast of California*, **DAVE G. HOUSER** specializes in cruise/luxury travel, personality, health, and history photography. He has been a runner-up for the Lowell Thomas Travel Journalist of the Year Award and was named the 1984 Society of American Travel Writers' Photographer of the Year.

Tracy City native **VIRGINIA HUGHES** is a law librarian at Miller & Martin LLP, and was chosen as one of the 2001 Best of Tennessee Exhibition Artists.

A graduate of Middle Tennessee State University, **BILLY KINGSLEY** has had images published by the *Tennessean, USA Today*, the *New York Times*, First Tennessee Bank, American General Financing Group, and Danlee Public Relations. He has won several national and regional awards from the University Photographers Association of America (UPAA) and the Council for the Advancement of Secondary Education (CASE), and he focuses on news, sports, travel, and culture photography.

Originally interested in fine art photography, **GARY LAYDA** is a photography instructor at Vanderbilt University Sarratt Center, Nashville Tech, and Middle Tennessee State University. Specializing in advertising, annual report, public relations, aerial, and stock photography, he has had images published in books, newspapers, and on television around the world, and has won local, national, and international awards for his work. A staff photographer for Metropolitan Government of Nashville since 1983, he does freelance work for such clients as Paine Webber, CBS, and Adelphia.

BUD LEE studied at the Columbia University School of Fine Arts in New York and the National Academy of Fine Arts. A self-employed photojournalist, he founded the Florida Photographers Workshop and the Iowa Photographers Workshop. His work can be seen in *Esquire, Life, Travel & Leisure, Rolling Stone*, the *Washington Post*, and *New York Times*, as well as in several Towery publications.

JUDI PARKS is an award-winning photojournalist living and working in the San Francisco Bay Area. Her work has been collected by museums and public collections in the United States and Europe, and her documentary series, *Home Sweet Home: Caring for America's Elderly*, was honored with the *Communication Arts-Design Annual* 1999 Award of Excellence for an unpublished series. Her images have appeared in numerous Towery publications.

The owner of Fine Grain Photo Lab, **KIM PAULSON** is originally from Ohio and has attended the School of Visual Arts in New York City. Her specialty is custom black-and-white printing and processing.

Focusing on advertising, corporate, and stock photography for such clients as DuPont, IBM, NationsBank, UPS, and Service Merchandise, **BOB SCHATZ** has had images published in several magazines including *Travel & Leisure, Business Week, Fortune*, and *Time*. The recipient of numerous ADDY awards, he has had images in several Towery publications.

JOHN SCHWEIKERT, a graduate of Vanderbilt University, is the owner of John Schweikert Photography, where he concentrates on people, places, and product photography.

For further information about the photographers appearing in *Nashville: Hills of Harmony*, please contact Towery Publishing.

Library of Congress Cataloging-in-Publication Data

Nashville : hills of harmony / introduction by Amy Grant : art direction by Karen Geary.
    p. cm.
Includes index.
  ISBN 1-58967-002-7 (alk. paper)
 1. Nashville (Tenn.)–Pictorial works. 2. Nashville (Tenn.)–Description and travel. 3. Nashville (Tenn.)–Economic conditions. 4. Business enterprises–Tennessee–Nashville. I. Grant, Amy. II. Geary, Karen, 1953–
F444.N243 N37 2001
976.8'55'00222–dc21

2001005915

TOWERY PUBLISHING
A DIVISION OF BARETZ PUBLISHING, LLC
THE TOWERY BUILDING • 1835 UNION AVENUE • MEMPHIS, TN 38104
www.towery.com

PUBLISHER: J. Robert Towery **EXECUTIVE PUBLISHER:** Jenny McDowell **SALES AND MARKETING:** Carol Culpepper, Gingo Spencer, Kim Wade **SALES MANAGER:** Bill Koons **PROJECT DIRECTORS:** Mary Helen Aldridge, Jennifer Bailey, Alexandria Dobkowski, Don Honeycutt, Doug Schwandner, Mark Tucker **EXECUTIVE EDITOR:** David B. Dawson **MANAGING EDITOR:** Lynn Conlee **SENIOR EDITORS:** Carlisle Hacker, Brian L. Johnston **PROJECT EDITOR/CAPTION WRITER:** Danna M. Greenfield **EDITORS:** Rebecca E. Farabough, Sabrina Richert, Ginny Yeager **PROFILE WRITER:** Heather Cochran **CREATIVE DIRECTOR:** Brian Groppe **PHOTOGRAPHY EDITOR:** Jonathan Postal **PHOTOGRAPHIC CONSULTANT:** Tom Stanford **PRODUCTION MANAGER:** Laurie Beck **PROFILE DESIGNERS:** Rebekah Barnhardt, Glen Marshall **PHOTOGRAPHY COORDINATOR:** Robin Lankford **PRODUCTION ASSISTANT:** Robert Parrish **SCANNING AND COLOR CORRECTION:** Eric Friedl, Darin Ipema, Mark Svetz, Rusty Timmons, Bill Towery **FILM PRODUCTION:** Jeff Burns, Michael Burns, Jamey Johnsen **PRINT COORDINATOR:** Beverly Timmons, printed in Hong Kong

Index of Profiles

Airport Ramada Inn & Suites 270

AmSouth Bank 218

Andersen 243

APAC-Tennessee, Inc. 232

Apex & Robert E. Lee Moving & Storage Company, Inc. 231

Aquinas College 234

Baptist Hospital 227

Battle Ground Academy 220

BellSouth Telecommunications, Inc. 256

Centex Homes 258

Citadel Communications Corporation 276

Comdata Corporation 240

Community Health Systems, Inc. 263

The Cromwell Group, Inc. 252

CRT, Custom Products, Inc. 246

Curb Records Inc. 272

Doubletree Hotel Nashville 248

Hardaway Construction Corporation 228

Harpeth Hall School 233

Hart Freeland Roberts, Inc. 226

HCA/TriStar Health System 236

Loews Vanderbilt Hotel 260

Nashville Area Chamber of Commerce 214

Nashville Business Journal 262

Nashville Electric Service 230

Renaissance Nashville Hotel 268

Saint Thomas Health Services 222

Sheraton Music City Hotel 264

Southwest Airlines 266

Tennessee Department of Environment and Conservation 269

Towery Publishing 280

Union Planters Bank 254

Vanderbilt Properties 244

Volunteer State Community College 242

XO Communications, Inc. 274

YMCA of Middle Tennessee 216